Geese
Geese as p
Geese Keeping, Care, Pros and Cons, Housing,
Diet and Health.
by

Roger Rodendale

Table of Contents

Introduction

For anyone who is looking for a pet or have economic reasons for owning poultry, geese are the perfect option. These birds are hardy, easy to maintain and can even make pretty good watch dogs for your home.

Geese have always been a part of our lives. Whether it is making their way into children's stories and poems or being the main attraction at your local park, geese have been known to live wonderful lives among humans.

They are fuss free eaters and will be happy with enough space to forage around. A majority of their diet includes grass. So if you have about a quarter of an acre of land, it is good enough for two geese. Of course, any lawn that is reasonably sized is a good option.

Besides that, geese are hardy animals that can adjust to most climatic changes. They will not fall ill easily if they are taken care of properly. Even the facilities that you have to provide for the birds such as nesting boxes are inexpensive, too.

The most important thing with geese is that you have to take care of them properly if you want to keep them disease free. That means you have to feed them well, give them a good amount of foraging space and provide them with proper hygiene and shelter.

For first timers, geese may be overwhelming, as they are larger than other poultry. You have to understand the correct way of handling them to keep them and yourself safe. It is also important to know why you want geese in the first place. If you want to raise them for commercial purposes, the responsibilities are quite different from raising them purely as pets.

Either way, geese can be extremely entertaining with their awkward personalities and their rather goofy demeanor. However, they are large creatures that can be powerful. So, making sure that learn everything you need to about raising them is very important.

This book will prepare you for the responsibility of having geese in your backyard. The book covers all the important topics like food, hygiene and health associated with geese.

The book draws from the experiences of people who have owned geese. So, all the tips provided are easy to apply and quite practical too.

The primary goal of the book is to become the complete guide that a beginner can use as they explore their relationship with their pet geese. The information provided covers all the issues from preparing your home for your pet geese to actually giving them a good life with you.

Here is hoping that you have a great time with your new pet. As long as you are able to provide for them, you can be assured that geese will make great pets.

Chapter 1: Introduction to Geese

Geese are waterfowl and are classified under the family Anatidae, under the Anserini tribe. Under this tribe you have three main categories, namely the Grey Geese or *Anser,* the black geese or the *Branta* and the White Geese or the *Chen.* There are many shelducks that have the name goose associated with them, but they do not belong to this species. The distantly related birds of the Anatidae family are swans and ducks, the former being significantly larger than geese and the latter being significantly smaller.

There are two genera of geese that are actually temporarily placed under the Anserinae family. They are actually speculated to belong to a separate sub species or may be related to shelducks. These two genera are the Cape Barren Goose or the *Cereopsis* and the prehistoric New Zealand goose or the *Cnemiornis.* It is believed that the Coscoroba swan or the two genera mentioned above are the most closely related ones to the true goose.

True geese are hard to classify into one genus based on fossil records. The fossils that have been found in North American are very dense and have documents of several species of the true geese that have been around since the Miocene era about 10 million years ago.

A type of true goose named *Anser atavus,* which translates to progenitor goose, has fossils that date back 12 million years. This species shares a lot of common traits with the swan. In addition, sub-fossil remains of several gooselike birds have been found in the Hawaiian Islands.

The word goose was derived from the Proto-Indo-European word Ghans. These roots gave birth to the old English word gos, which was used as ges and ganders in plural from. From these old English words, we have derived the modern terms goose, geese gander and gosling.

The root word gave birth to several other references to the goose such as goes, gies and guoske in Fisian, Gans, Ganse and Ganter in

New High German, gans in Dutch, gate in Albanian, hamsa or hamsi in Sanskrit and so on.

In modern times the word goose usually refers to the female, while the term gander is used to refer to the male. The young geese that haven't fledged yet are known as gosling.

The collective noun for a group of geese is a gaggle. When in flight, a group of geese is referred to as a skein, wedge or team. If they fly really close to one another, they are known as a plump of geese.

What is most interesting is the transition of the goose from a wild bird that was usually hunted for meat to a popular choice for a pet or a poultry bird. Geese have been among human beings for several years now and have been referred to in cultural elements such as poetry and stories.

The next section delves into the details of the history and origin of the goose.

1. The origins of geese
Most of the domestic geese in the European, North African and West Asian regions are descendants of the graylag goose, which is also known as *anser anser*.

In East Asia, the domesticated goose is a descendant of the swan goose or the *Anser cygnoides*. This species is known as the Chinese goose. Both types of geese have been introduced in recent times in more parts of the world, including North America and Australia. There is a chance that there are hybrids or either species in both areas.

You can see a clear distinction between the Chinese and European Geese with the large knob that is present at the base of the bill in the former species. Of course you can see some variations in the hybrids that are common for both species.

In his book, the Variation of Animals and Plants under domestication, Charles Darwin mentions that the domestication of geese dates back more than 4000 years ago. Fossils that are this old, or slightly more, have been unearthed in Egypt. The fossils indicate that the size is larger in the case of the ancient domesticated geese.

They weigh up to 10 kilos in comparison to the fossils of the wild swan geese and the wild graylag geese that weigh between 3.4-4.1 kilos. It is believed that the larger geese were domesticated on purpose.

The larger size has led to the domesticated geese having a rather different body stricture in comparison to the wild species. In the case of wild geese, the posture is more horizontal and the rear is slim. On the other hand, in the case of the domesticated geese, they have fat deposits near the rear of their body, making it appear bulky. This added weight near the tail makes the posture of the bird a lot more upright.

Domesticated geese are unable to fly due to their unique structure. This is probably why they were domesticated in the first place. Now, in the case of domesticated geese, the usual response to any threat is running and extensive wing flapping. While doing this, they may get their feet of the ground momentarily. This is the maximum extent of flight in these birds in most cases.

Another reason for the preference given to the larger geese is that they are capable of laying several eggs. While a wild goose typically lays close to 12 eggs in a year, the species of geese that have been selected for domestication can lay up to 50 eggs each year.

Any change in the plumes of the domestic goose in comparison to the wild ones is not constant. There are various colors that you can expect. In most cases, the ones with fewer brown tones were chosen for domestication. So, you will see that domestic geese usually have markings on their body or may only have white feathers all over.

It is possible, however, that some of them retain the natural plumes. For instance, the Toulouse goose that is domesticated in the modern day resembles and almost looks identical to the greylag goose in terms of the coloration, with a slight difference in the structure.

Most commonly, people like to have white geese in their backyard because the look a lot better and seem to be very "dressed" thanks to the inconspicuous down feathers that give the plumes a ruffled appearance. It is not just in the modern day but since the time of the

Roman Empire that white geese have been given most preference as pets.

Most people like to have a goose as a backyard pet because of the size of the eggs that they produce. These eggs are edible and can weigh about 170 grams each. They can be cooked just like chicken eggs. The advantage is that these eggs have more yolk and are denser in terms of consistency. In terms of taste, the goose egg is a gamier version of the chicken egg.

Security is one of the reasons why people have often opted to have geese in their backyards. They have a call that is extremely loud. You will hear a loud call from a goose in case of any small or unusual movement. In fact, these birds are so alert that they were used by the VNAF in the late 1950s in the Southern part of Vietnam in order to guard aircrafts when they were parked at night.

Despite domestication, this species of geese will breed with wild geese as well, as they have descended from the wild graylag geese. This leads to interesting colorations or may lead to offspring that resemble one of the parents. In the case of mixed colors, you will normally see a blend of gray and white feathers.

Geese in mythology and fiction

Since geese have been a part of human civilization for several centuries, it is natural that they have made their way into mythology and literature.

One of the most significant references is in Greek mythology, where the bird has been linked to the Goddess of love, Aphrodite. According to one mythological tale, Aphrodite was welcomed by Charites or Graces in Roman Literature when she first came ashore. The latter's chariot was drawn by several geese.

Of course, everyone knows the popular Mother Goose stories that have been passed on through the ages by farmwives. The "Goose that laid golden eggs" is one of the most popular stories that children have been told. This is a story that warns people of the perils of being too greedy

The Vise or the Musee Regional d'Archeologie et d'Histoire de Vise discusses the references and the images of domestic geese that have been used in classical antiquity. In fact, this discussion that was held in the year 1994 also has a separate chapter that talks about the several references to domestic geese that have been made in popular folklore worldwide.

2. Types of geese

According to the FAO or the Food and Agriculture Organization of the United Nations, there are about 96 breeds of geese that are found worldwide. Of these, only a few have been chosen as poultry birds or pets. The rest of them have not risen to as much popularity because they are not the most economically important birds. They are either low in numbers worldwide or have been rejected because of their limited distribution geographically.

Several new breeds have arisen consistently because of cross breeding. There are several species that are the result of experiments conducted by companies and individuals who specialize in breeding geese.

In this chapter, we will discuss the best options that you can choose from when you decide to bring a goose into your home as a utility bird or as a pet.

a. Chinese geese

The Chinese goose has been classified as *Anser cygnoides.* There are 20 breeds and counting of this type of goose. They are very popular in North America and in Europe and are known for the classic knob that you will find at the base of the beak.

You will find several varieties in terms of plumage. There are white and brown colorations that you will find in these birds. However, the white variety is one of the most popular ones. The popularity of the brown colored varieties is declining rapidly because of the inability to use them for meat. These birds have pin feathers that are colored, making them less attractive as a game bird in comparison to the white feathered birds.

In the case of the white birds, you will see orange colored beaks, shanks and knobs. In the case of the brown varieties, the shanks are orange in color. The beak and the knob, however, have a distinct dark green or even black coloration.

The knob is not only a distinguishing feature but is also very important in sexing the birds. At the age of 6-8 weeks, they help determine the gender of the bird. In the case of the male birds, the knob is a lot more prominent in comparison to the female birds.

Chinese geese as much smaller in size and will weigh about 5 kilos in the case of males and about 4 kilos in the case of the females. This breed is very popular because of the large yield of eggs. There have been several reports of these birds laying about 100 eggs in just one breeding season. This season lasts for just 5 months in a year, from February to June. The average yield is 60 eggs, which is quite impressive. Each egg weighs 120 grams, which can be considered larger than the eggs laid by other species of geese.

They are not commonly used in the production of meat because they have a very small body conformation. In addition to that, the meat yield itself is quite low for these birds.

These birds are not popular in breeding programs either, as they are not considered a pure breed. What they are popular for is their ability to be great guard birds. They also have very strong legs that can take them across long distances in case they need to forage. This is one of the reasons why the species has spread from China all the way to countries like India and Siberia. They are known to travel for long distances in search of food. This quality also means that they are hardy birds that can survive in different climatic conditions.

b. Czechoslovakian white
These birds have been classified as *Anser anser.* They are known for their trademark white plumage that is beautifully contrasted by the orange shanks and beak.

These birds have also been referred to as the Bohemian goose in some cases.

The body size is quite small, with the males growing up to about 5 kilos and the females weighing about 4 kilos on average. These birds are also extremely popular as poultry birds because of the high egg production. They normally lay about 45 eggs in one breeding season. These eggs are also counted among the larger goose eggs because they can weigh about 140 grams each.

They are very popular as breeding geese. They are considered a pure breed. This is one of the common reasons why the females belonging to this species are very useful in producing cross breeds that can be commercially used with great rates of success.

c. Embden

These birds are also classified as *Anser Anser*. They differ from the Czech white in the type of feathering. These birds have very tight feathering in comparison to the Czech whites.

The shanks and the beak in these birds are also very brightly colored. Sexing in these birds is relatively easy and can be done based on the coloration on the goslings. The males have a lighter grey plumage in comparison to the females. You will notice this distinct difference in the coloration when the birds are as young as three weeks of age.

The Embden goose is popular in North America and Europe and has been domesticated for several years. These are the larger varieties of geese. The male birds can weigh about 10 kilos while females go up to 9 kilos.

In terms of egg yield, these birds are considered moderate, as they lay about 40 eggs in one breeding season. These eggs weigh about 170 grams.

Embden geese are popular among those who want to breed or raise geese for meat production. These birds are heavy and are valuable in the production of meat. This is one of the reasons why they are chosen for breeding programs as well.

In the case of meat yielding birds, it is the male that is usually chosen to breed with other species of geese to yield a suitable cross breed for commercial use.

d. Hyoyan goose

This breed is classified as *Anser cygnoides*. This breed finds its origins in China in the Changtu county located in the Liaoning province. These geese are quite different from regular Chinese geese because their bodies are relatively lighter and the yield of eggs is a lot higher.

This breed is a popular choice for domestication because it can lay up to 200 eggs in one breeding season. In terms of appearance, these birds tend to have orange shanks and beaks. The coloration however can differ quite significantly.

In the year 1981, a genetic selection program in the Animal and Veterinary Institute of Tie Ling in China used about 500 geese of this breed. The main focus of this program was egg production. Out of the 500 birds, the ones that were not entirely white and the ones that lacked an opening in the eyelid were rejected.

The preferred birds were able to lay eggs when they were about 240 days old. On average, they produced between 90 and 210 eggs in each breeding season. A sizeable 10 percent of the selected geese were able to produce 200-210 eggs in each breeding season. Each egg weighed between 120-210 gams.

The weight of a fully-grown adult male bird was about 4.5 kilos, while that of a fully grown female bird was about 3 kilos. Other interesting points that were noted about this breed were the ability to resist extremely cold conditions and also the ability to use rough fodder efficiently.

These birds also have the knob that is commonly seen in geese that originate in this part of the world.

e. Kuban
Kuban geese are classified as *Anser cygnoides.* This breed was developed by crossing Chinese geese with Gorki geese. They were developed in south Russia in the Kuban Agricultural institute.

These birds are not preferred for the production of meat. This is mainly because they are brown in color with pin feathers that are very dark. Therefore, they have an unpleasant appeal, which makes them less popular for consumption as food.

The shanks of these birds are the typical orange in color. The knob and the beak, on the other hand, are usually dark green or black in color.

The fully-grown male weighs about 5.2 kilos while a fully grown female weighs about 4.8 kilos.

One of the biggest advantages of this breed of geese is that they are able to produce about 60 eggs in one breeding season, which is relatively high. Each egg weighs about 120 grams.

Because of the high yield, the females of this breed are usually preferred for cross breeding. The goal of most cross breeding programs is to produce pure white offspring so that the poor body conformation of this breed of geese can be overcome. Such birds are commercially very likely to succeed.

f. Landes
These birds are classified as *Anser Anser*. The male and the female birds have grey plumage. The shanks and beaks range from yellow to orange in color.

This breed was developed in France but gained popularity in several countries. They are very popular in Hungary because they are able to produce Foie Gras or Fatty liver.

Many lines of this breed have been produced particularly for their ability to produce Foie Gras. This breed of geese was produced with the white Toulouse goose. However, they closely resemble Greylag geese in coloration. They differ from the wild geese mostly in size. The male birds usually weigh about 6 kilos while the females weigh about 5 kilos.

Annual egg production is moderate at about 40 eggs per breeding season, per female. Each egg weighs about 170 grams, which is quite desirable.

g. Pilgrim geese
These geese are classified as *Anser anser*. They are among the most popular breeds in North America. These breeds were recognized officially in the year 1939. However, these birds are declining in popularity over the years.

The most unique quality of the Pilgrim goose is the sexual dimorphism. The adult male has grey plumes while the adult female has white plumes.

These birds are considered a medium weight breed. The adults will weigh about 6 kilos when they are fully grown and females are known to weigh up to 5 kilos.

The reason for the rapid decline in commercial value of these birds is the low egg yield. On average, each female will produce only up to 30 eggs in each breeding season.

h. Pomeranian geese
These geese are classified as *Anser Anser*. This breed was developed in the north western region of Poland. They are, however, found in southern Sweden and the North eastern part of Germany as well.

These birds have three distinct colorations- white, grey and mixed. In all the three varieties, the color of the shanks and the beak is orange. These geese are known for their solid build.

The male birds will usually weigh about 6 kilos and the female will weigh about 5 kilos. Egg production in each breeding season is average, with each female laying about 40 eggs that will weigh about 170 grams.

i. Synthetic Ukrainian
These birds are classified as *Anser Anser*. These birds are among the new strains of geese that have been synthetically developed in Bokri at the Ukrainian Poultry Research Centre.

These birds are also sexually dimorphic by the time they are about eight weeks old. The males have primary grey feathers while the females are primarily white.

These birds are counted among the medium sized geese. The male will, on average, grow up to about 6 kilos while the female will grow up to about 5.4 kilos.

In terms of egg production, these birds are fairly good. In every breeding season, you can expect each female to lay between 45 and 55 eggs.

j. White Hungarian
These birds are classified as *Anser Anser*. As the name suggests, these birds have white plumes. The shanks and the beaks are usually orange in color. Physically, these birds resemble the White Italian Geese quite closely. The biggest difference is that these birds have a lower egg production.

This breed has been developed to produce improved lines that are mainly used for feather production. They are also used to produce cross breeds that can provide good quality meat and Foie Gras.

They are medium sized birds, with the male weighing about 5.5 kilos and the female weighing about 4.7 kilos. Normally, the female will produce about 45 eggs in one breeding season. Each egg will weigh about 160 grams.

k. White Italian Geese
These geese are classified as *Anser Anser.* They are among the top breeds in Europe, as they are able to form local stocks. This is also among the best researched breeds in Europe.

Extensive publications about this bird have been maintained since the 1960s for genetic selection at the Koluda Weilka Experimental Station in Poland. They have been mentioned under genetic selection, where several separate lines of females and males have been developed.

In the first ten days of hatching it is possible to sex the goslings, as the male birds have lighter plumes in comparison to the females. In the case of the adults, the plumes are entirely white. The shanks and the beak are orange in color.

These are larger sized birds, with the male weighing about 7 kilos and the female weighing about 6.5 kilos.

These birds have a fairly high egg production, with each female producing about 65 eggs in one breeding season. The range of the weight of the eggs is from 160 to 180 kilos.

Of all the *Anser Anser* type of geese, the White Italian is considered to be the highest in terms of egg yield. As a result, this is a popular choice for cross breeding programs. Usually, these birds are used to produce commercially successful lines that are not only used for egg production but for good quality meat production as well.

3. Habitat
Geese are geographically distributed in the Palearctic region. Among the eight biogeographic realms on the Earth's surface, the Palearctic realm is the largest. It is distributed across Asia, northern

Africa, Europe, the northern part of the Himalayan foothills and the central and northern parts of the Arabian Peninsula.

There are several lakes and rivers that flow in these places, giving birth to freshwater eco-regions that are ideal for birds like geese. These rivers were, in fact, a reliable source for water for many civilizations that used irrigation successfully for agriculture.

Geese and its sub-species are widely distributed in Norway, Iceland, Sweden, Finland, northern Russia, the Baltic States, Romania and eastern Hungary.

They breed naturally in Austria, Czech Republic, Slovakia, Denmark, United Kingdom and Germany. You will find an eastern race of geese that extends from China to a large portion of Asia.

The European geese usually migrate towards the northern parts of African and the Mediterranean areas. The birds that are found in the Asian region will migrate to Azerbaijan, Baluchistan, Pakistan, Iran, North India, China and Bangladesh.

In the Northern part of America, you will see feral geese that are located in certain areas and also vagrants that you will see outside the regular range that you find geese in. Greylag geese are surprisingly found in New Zealand in the wild. It is believed that these geese escaped from the farm areas. A similar phenomenon occurred in Australia as well. You will see feral birds in the eastern and southeastern part of the country.

The distribution varies based on the season and the biological cycle of the birds. For instance, during their breeding quarter, these birds are usually seen near lakes or on islands that extend a little into the sea.

During the breeding season, the birds prefer to live in dense ground that has a good cover of rushes, heather, bushes, willow thickets and reeds.

Larger areas are preferred when they are breeding. Usually, they will choose areas that have at least five acres of grazing areas and open water. This helps them get the nutrition that is needed during the stressful breeding season.

The distribution of the birds changes when winter approaches. They are usually seen in freshwater marshes, steppes, flooded fields, bogs, pastures, salt marshes and estuaries. They are also seen quite frequently in areas that have water such as rivers, streams and lakes.

They will frequent agricultural areas where they can feed on crops like rice, beans, winter grains and others. They move at dusk or at nightfall to shoals, sandbanks, mud-banks and lakes that are secluded. One of the most spectacular sights is the congregation of several immature geese in the Baltic Sea on the Rone Islands. These birds come in to molt there.

Basically, in the winter months they need a habitat that is rich in grass and other shrubs for grazing. They also need to have enough open water that they can consume.

Unfortunately, in Great Britain the popularity of the bird as a breeding bird has declined over the years. Large populations have moved to the north to breed in the Outer Hebrides. You will also see a few birds in the northern part of mainland Scotland.

During the 20th Century, few feral populations have developed in other parts of England. Re-colonization is one of the reasons why these birds have moved to more areas of England. They have constantly come into contact with urban populations due to this.

Chapter 2: Bringing Geese Home

If you are entirely sure that you want to bring geese home, the next step is to figure out why you want to bring them home in the first place.

Following that, you can look for a reliable breeder who will be able to provide you with the breed or type of goose that you are looking for.

It is always better to buy geese in pairs. Pairs of the same gender are a good idea if they have been raised together. You also get a chance for possible breeding during mating season.

1.Why geese make great pets

Geese can be an important part of a pasture. They make great companions and besides that they have several other behaviors that can actually be of a lot of benefit to humans. Here are a few reasons why bringing a goose home is a good idea:

a. Most efficient lawn mowers

Geese love to eat grass and certain herbaceous plants. This helps control the growth of grass automatically and also reduces the amount of weed that grows in your pasture.

While you may be able to get rid of most excessive growth of grass and weed manually, the advantage with geese is that they will allow you to actually reach out to spots like ditches and also along the rows of fencing.

Several weed crops like orchards, strawberries, cotton, etc. can be controlled if you have geese on your farm. If you have a pond, they are also useful in getting rid of pond weeds like water lily and water hyacinth.

If you want to bring home geese particularly for weed control you will need about 50 adults per 2.5 acres. If you just want them to graze lightly, 20 adults are good enough.

b. Utility birds

Geese are raised for meat and egg production on many farms. Of course, if you are looking for companion animals, the idea of meat production is definitely out of the question

Historically, however, geese have been raised for meat, as they are large birds. This is one of the reasons why the bigger birds were selected for domestication in ancient civilizations.

Certain breeds are raised to produce foie gras or fatty liver. Most others are raised for egg production. As we discussed in the previous chapter, geese can lay up to 100 eggs in one breeding season. The large eggs are also extremely wholesome.

c. Great pets

Geese tend to get very attached to their owners. They are also highly intelligent and affectionate birds. If you breed geese on your farm, it is likely that the young ones will also accept you as the parent. In particular, geese are known to become great, loving pets.

These birds are not the best option if you are living in a residential area, as they tend to get extremely loud. That can become a nuisance to the neighbors. So if homes in the neighborhood are in close proximity to one another, then getting geese is not the best idea.

Even if you do not want to breed the geese and want to purely raise them as pets, it is a good idea to have a group of females. A flock of males can lead to aggression and is generally not recommended.

You must at least have a pair of geese if you want them to have a healthy and a happy development under your care.

d. Best guard animals
Geese have the unique ability to learn sounds. That makes them capable of identifying sounds that are common on your farm or in your household. So, even with the slightest deviation from normal, these birds will be completely alert and will make loud noises when there is a new person or even animal in your premises.

These birds were used by the Romans as a means to detect enemies that were approaching. They were believed to be more reliable than watchdogs. They are extremely alert and can spot a threat in an instant.

Remember that breeds that are raised to be guard animals can be a nuisance in a residential area. These breeds include the Chinese goose and the Pomeranian Goose that will honk at every passerby or animal. The alarm that they sound is extremely loud and can persist all day long. This is followed by rigorous wing flapping and a lot of commotion to scare the potential threat away.

2. Goose requirements
If you are bringing geese home, you need to make sure that your space is equipped to accommodate these birds. Remember that geese can grow up to be very large birds that need enough physical and mental stimulation in order to be healthy. Here are a few basic requirements of geese:

- Geese require a good amount of grass. A major part of their diet constitutes grass and clover. The general requirement of geese is about a quarter of an acre per pair of geese. You need to make sure that they have access to good quality grass throughout the year.

- They need proper healthcare. This means including a good program for vaccination and also maintenance of the premises to ensure that there is no chance for bacteria, fungi or other microorganisms to thrive.

- They need to have proper shelter. Even if you are unable to build expensive pens with perches and nest boxes, your geese can be maintained in great condition. All you need to do is provide them with shelter such as a shed that has ample ventilation.

- The enclosure that you keep your geese in should be completely predator proof. These birds are prey birds and can fall victim to several predators. You also need to keep wild birds and rodents away from the enclosure, as they can be carriers of several diseases. Fencing is very important if you decide to raise geese on your farm or in your backyard.

- Geese require good nutrition. If you are unsure about what to feed your birds, you may consult your vet to provide you with tips. Poor nutrition can lead to serious health issues including bumblefoot.

- They have to have a water source available. While it is not mandatory to have a pond, you need to keep in mind that about 10% of their time each day is spent on water. If you are not able to give them access to a pond or lake, a plastic tub or a pit tub with water is good enough for them. If you plan to breed geese, particularly, you need to make sure that water is available, as most geese breed readily only when this is the case.

- Shade is a must if you live in the warmer part of the world. Now, the shelter that you provide them with can be of great use. In addition to that, having trees or areas with makeshift roofs can be necessary to ensure that your birds do not suffer from issues like overheating.

The requirements change with the type of breed that you bring home. For instance, a heavier breed will require more water depth in comparison to the lighter breeds. You need to make sure that you study the breed that you are bringing home correctly.

Raising a healthy flock also requires you to choose its members carefully. Sourcing your geese from the right people can be of great help. The next section will give you all the tips you need when choosing a goose for your home.

3. Obtaining geese

You have the option of either getting eggs and goslings or adult birds when you decide to bring geese into your home. The best option is to look for a breeder who will be able to sell you eggs or adult birds.

Here are a few things that you need to keep in mind whether you are buying eggs and goslings or adult geese.

a. Buying eggs and goslings

You will be able to find the eggs of pure bred geese on sale on most farms. However, it is good to note that reputable breeders will rarely sell off the eggs. As geese eggs tend to have a random rate of fertility, a breeder may not sell eggs to you. They will actually need the eggs themselves.

This also means that those who are willing to sell the eggs may do so at a high price. You will be able to find advertisements of eggs that are about to hatch in newspapers. You can even look up the websites of local farms to get updated information on eggs on sale.

The breed may be known in cases of purebred geese. There are also chances of hybrids. But there are a few details that you must ask for before you bring a goose egg home:

- How old are the eggs?
- What are the storing methods that they use?
- Have the eggs been incubated already or not?

It is not recommended to buy eggs because of the risks involved in transporting them. They tend to get shaken up a lot, which means that they are at the risk of arriving with low chances for survival. They may also develop very low hatchability.

You will rarely find goslings of purely bred geese. This is because the assessment of the quality is not possible that early. Now, most breeders will choose to keep the best goslings for the production of new stock each year. They will be able to find goslings that are of good breeder quality, exhibition quality or pet quality. The ones that are of pet quality are put up for sale in most cases.

Of course, the prices of the geese will differ based on the quality and you can ask for the one that you like. If you have any specifications about quality, it is a good idea to wait until they are well grown and you are sure of their.quality. You will be able to find good quality adult birds on sale from the month of August with most non-commercial breeders.

b. Buying adult birds
You can identify the adult birds with their second feathers. This happens usually around the time the birds are 16 weeks old. At this time they are not really sexually mature and will grow and develop for some time.

You can obtain birds past their prime age to keep in your backyards or as pets. It is not advisable to buy a female with a distended abdomen if you are interested in egg production. These birds tend to produce eggs with a double yolk. That means that they are infertile.

If you are interested in breeding, it is necessary to get females that are about three to four years old. In the wild, geese will not lay eggs until they are about three years old. However, domestic geese may lay eggs in the first year, but it is advised that you wait until they are two years old. That is when the eggs will be of their full size.

You can also get a two year old gander. You have to ask the breeder about the hatching duration of the male. If he has hatched late, there are chances that he will not be able to breed. On the other hand, early hatched male yearlings tend to have a better ability to breed.

Buying from an experienced breeder means that your bird can be sexed before purchase. They will be able to identify the gender of the bird from the behavior and voice quite easily.

It is always a good idea to look for a breeder who works in your state or country at least. Shipping geese can be a hassle, as you may not find licensed professional carriers to carry livestock.

c. Determining the quality of the birds

If you are looking for purebred geese, there are specific breed faults that you can do some research about. Here are a few criteria that you can use to assess the quality of the bird that you are about to bring home:

The color, size and shape

It is common for birds to develop their adult feathers by the time they are about 18 weeks old. You will also be able to see a well-developed body shape in these birds. Of course, when you are opting for the heavier breeds, there is a chance of a growth spurt and you never know how big they can get.

The best thing to do would be to take a look at the parent birds. The offspring will, more or less, be like the parent birds. When you are buying pure breeds, you will be able to find standard descriptions of these birds on official websites of dedicated clubs. Make sure you read them well and ensure that the bird you are purchasing fits those standards.

General faults to look out for

While there are several breed-specific faults in geese, you must also look out for some general faults that will make it possible to assess the quality of the bird you are about to purchase:

- You must never accept a bird that is delivered to you in a cardboard box or literally parceled up to your doorstep. In case you do receive such a package after an online order, make sure the box is weighed. If it seems light, the bird could be infected by worms, could be underfed or could be severely unwell.

- When you hold the bird, make sure the eyes are checked. If the eye is not of the right color and if they look watery or have any discharge, it is a sign of illnesses. There must be no opaque growth on the pupil that may compromise the health. This will affect the behavior of your geese extensively.

- Make sure you check the feet of the bird. There must not be any swelling in the ankles and the hocks. The bird should also have straight toes and the underside of the web in younger birds should not have any callus development.

- Let the bird move around and observe it. If you see any irregularity in the movement, it is a sign of poor eyesight.

- You can even see structural deformities such as a wry tail or a curved back. Any deformity of the bill may be seen immediately or may develop later on.

- The wings of the bird should be set properly. If there are slipped wings, especially in males, the bird will be incapable of performing activities like breeding.

- Keep an eye on the interaction of the bird with the breeder or the owner. When called, does the bird run away or does he come to the owner. The more responsive the bird is to humans, the easier it will be to tame him to settle into your home.

It is best that you buy birds that are 16 weeks old or older, as birds younger than this age do not show possible health issues that could pose a threat to their well-being. If the breeder is able to offer a health certificate, it can be of great value.

d. Advantages of buying purebred geese
If you can figure out which breed suits your requirements, it is a good idea to purchase from an established breeder who sells purebred geese. The advantages are as follows:

- The bird will conform to the standards that have been established for each pure breed.

26

- These birds will most often come with an identity number, which will help you maintain proper health records.

- You will know the characteristics of the breed and can seek advice accordingly.

- It is possible to compare your bird to existing samples of this breed.

- You will know the exact breeding history of the bird that you are bringing home. For instance, you will know if the birds are related or unrelated.

- You have the advantage of knowing the exact age and gender of each bird.

- In case there has been a mistake in the delivery, a reputed breeder will take the bird back.

- Management advice is easy to obtain from a breeder who will have ample experience.

- You can handle the birds easily, as they probably have been hand raised. That also makes it easy to check the birds for health.

- Worming and health advice is easily available.

- You will be able to get the appropriate bedding, housing and feed for each bird.

- The behavior of the bird is known. That way you know if you are ready for this breed or not.

Make sure that you only deal with a breeder who has a good reputation. You can even visit the premises to check if the birds have been maintained properly or not. If you see shabby enclosures and birds that look poor in health, it is not a good idea to buy from such a breeder.

e. Adopting geese

Another option that you have with obtaining geese is to adopt one. With these birds, you can expect good companionship. However, there may be a history of ill management and even abuse in some cases. That means you will have to learn how to handle each bird before actually bringing one home. Egg and meat production may or may not be an option with these birds.

Here are a few tips to adopt a goose for your home:

- Ask for the adoption fees. In most cases, shelters will charge you up to $35 or £20 for each bird to ensure that the maintenance and medical charges are met.

- Check for the tests that have been conducted on the bird. In some shelters, the bird is quarantined before handing them over to the adopting family. You can even ask for tests conducted for parasites and common health disorders.

- Confirm if they ship the bird to you. Some shelters may not do this as a policy. However, they will be willing to offer a 2-3 hour ride to meet potential owners halfway. It is however a good idea to pick the bird up from the shelter.

- Make sure that you carry a large sized carrier for your new bird. Most shelters will not allow you to take the bird in a cardboard box or carrier. Line the carrier with soft bedding and choose a large enough carrier to make the ride less stressful for your bird.

- A water source is necessary for the bird that you are driving home. Food is not a necessity unless the shelter is more than 6 hours away. This will prevent issues like vomiting and choking.

- In case the trip is longer than 6 hours, you can add about ¼ cup of some food to the water dish every 5 hours. The food must be enough to keep the stomach calm but not so much that that the bird will fall ill.

- The door of the vehicle that you are transporting the bird in should never be opened. If the bird is in a state of panic, he will jump right out. Even windows must be kept closed at all times.

- Most of the shelters will not allow the birds to be carried in an attached truck bed and will insist that you keep the bird inside your vehicle the whole time.

- If you are travelling during the warmer months, air conditioning is mandatory. Keeping it on at room temperature will help keep the bird comfortable throughout the trip.

- Make sure that you read the adoption contract thoroughly before you sign it. That will help you understand the house checking process and the conditions for retrieval of the bird in case the shelter finds that the bird is not maintained properly. You will also have a clear understanding of the conditions to return the bird if you are unable to keep them for various reasons.

You can look up the website of local shelters if you are interested in adoption. Most of them will have an updated website. So, any bird that is listed there is most likely going to be available to you.

If you spot a bird that you want to bring home, make sure that you call them immediately. You can keep the bird on hold after paying the adoption fee. Usually the birds are kept on hold for a maximum of seven days. After that, if you are unable to pick the bird up, your adoption fee will not be refunded. The bird will be relisted and you will have to pay the adoption fee yet again if you are still interested.

Adoption is a great idea because there are several birds that are turned in each month or even week because owners are unable to provide them with the basic requirements. If you are considering adoption, make sure that you are fully prepared to take complete care of the bird.

4. Planning for geese

Whether you are buying or adopting a goose to keep on a farm or in your home, it is necessary to plan well in advance to ensure that you are able to keep them and maintain them well. Here are a few tips that will help you when you are planning to bring a goose home:

- First learn if geese are allowed in the area that you live in. It is a good idea to consult with a municipal agency to learn about the regulations. Some zones may require a license to obtain geese. Others may have regulations with respect to the type of enclosure, the distance from the property boundaries, the number of birds you are allowed to keep, pen size, etc.

- Make sure that the fencing, feed and the housing is sorted before you obtain the geese. If the enclosures are not in place, you need to be prepared for droppings all over your yard or pasture.

- If you have children at home, make sure that they are old enough to understand what it means to have a goose. Geese are easily spooked by loud behavior or sudden approaches. If the child is unable to manage his or her behavior around the goose, you are putting the child at great risk. Geese are large birds and tend to bite or kick when they are startled. This will cause serious injuries.

- If you are bringing geese into a residential area, make sure that you consult your neighbors. If you are bringing breeds like Chinese or African geese into your home, they can be extremely noisy. If the neighbors complain about your birds, you must either be prepared to make the necessary arrangements or may have to give the goose away.

- If you are a beginner in the world of geese, start small. You can begin with a pair. Even if you have experience with ducks or chickens, remember that geese are very different in their needs as well as their behavior.

- If you have a purpose for bringing the birds home, make sure that they fit the bill. You can discuss the purpose with your breeder to find a suitable bird for you.

- Remember that a goose is a commitment. They live for as long as 20 years and you are responsible for the health and well-being of the bird. Therefore, avoid any impulse buying with respect to geese.

- Before you decide to bring a goose home, it is advisable to meet previous goose owners to understand the body language that geese respond to and how they respond to it. They are extremely sensitive to body language and if you are not able to provide them with calm and relaxed energy, you will need to work on it.

- In case you decide to buy a goose at an auction, it is mandatory to have someone who is a specialist in these birds accompany you. That way, you will be able to assess the health, gender, age and even the breed of the birds correctly before purchasing one.

- When you are buying goslings it is best not to buy from auctions, as there can be several health issues. Buy them from a point of supply. You will require addition supplies and facilities in order to raise goslings.
- There is also the slight chance that goslings have developed gizzard worm if they have been raised on grass.

When you are purchasing geese, take some time to analyze the requirements and the responsibility of bringing home these birds. They can become extremely attached to you and will make the best companions, provided you can provide them with everything they need.

5. Introducing geese to an existing flock

If you already have a flock or pair and want to introduce a new goose into it, you need to understand that this not very easy to do. Geese can get very competitive and aggressive, especially during mating season.

A word of caution; geese will form extremely strong bonds with their companions, especially when the breeding season arrives. They can become very aggressive with a new comer that is introduced during this period.

That said, there are some safe ways of introducing geese to a flock without any damage to the new bird or the existing bird.

With poultry birds like chickens, it is advised that you give them a lot of space to ensure that the ones that are the lowest in the pecking order are able to escape from fights and dominance rituals.

However, this is not true in the case of geese. The first thing you need to keep in mind is the season. Only make introductions in summers to make sure that you are not disturbing the breeding season.

Remove a gander from the flock and place all the females in a small enclosure. They should not be able to roam around freely. Then, you will introduce the new female during the night.

The next day, you will keep an eye on them. Since these birds are forced to be in one another's company they may not be thrilled, but when they have less space to move and with the gander out of the flock, the chances of fights are fewer.

Of course, there will be several squabbles in the flock. That is natural and will be gone in a few days or weeks. When this stops, you can allow the geese to roam around on the pasture as a group.

When you notice that the birds are comfortable with one another, the gander can be reintroduced. The gander will also be introduced at night. Generally, the gander will accept all the geese and will settle down peacefully.

It is not recommended to introduce an adult gander into a flock. Instead, you may consider replacing an existing gander. You may want to change the gander due to his age, the inability to breed, etc. If you are replacing multiple ganders, it needs to be done at the same time.

Usually, introducing goslings into a flock is much easier. Geese tend to be generous when it comes to adopting a new gosling into the flock.

6. Raising a mixed flock
It is common for people to be interested in raising a mixed flock of birds that include ducks, geese, chickens and others. On a farmyard,

each bird has a different purpose. Of course, they can also be extremely entertaining.

The one issue with a mixed flock is the chance of squabbles and fights between the birds. When you are dealing with large birds and small birds on one property, it can lead to very serious repercussions.

In flocks, a pecking order is pre-decided. One of them leads while the others follow in order from the strongest to the meekest. If there is any change in the environment or in case a new bird is introduced, this pecking order will be disturbed. This is harder to manage when you mix species, so you need to make sure that you follow a few simple tips that will reduce the complications of raising a mixed flock.

- **Make sure that the gender ratios are in check**
  A flock becomes unhappy when there are too many males and very few females. In the absence of enough females, the male birds will begin to fight to assert dominance. Each species has a different requirement. For instance, Geese will need about three females per male, turkeys will need ten females per male, chickens will need eight hens per rooster, etc.

- **Give the birds enough space**
  The birds will need to have enough room so that they can forage and move around comfortably. One thing that is very important is for the birds in the flock to have enough space to escape from bossy members of each flock.

  Research shows that birds that are free range are a lot more harmonious. About 10 feet of pasture per bird is required as a general rule.

  At nightfall, the resting areas differ. For example, birds like turkeys and chickens require space to roost at night. But in the case of waterfowl, this is not a necessity. For the birds that need roosting, you have to build sturdy roosts so that they can feel safe and secure.

With night shelters, the major requirement is to ensure that the birds are safe from rain and wind. They must also have ample space to rest without the shelter getting too crowded.

- **If you have small birds, make a sanctuary for them**
On most farms, geese play the role of guardian birds. They are kept to protect smaller poultry like chickens. This is one of the most cost effective ways to keep your small poultry safe from predators like cats and skunks.

  If you have guardian geese, they need to have a separate enclosure at night. The smaller birds should have ample space to escape when the geese spring into action in the presence of a predator.

  You may simply provide a blocked off area or a few roosts that the birds can live happily in.

- **Make sure the birds are introduced properly**
The hardest part is introducing birds to one another, unless you know the temperament and understand the behavior perfectly.

  The age gap is one of the most important factors to consider. In the case of birds like chickens, they must not be introduced until they are 8 weeks old if the flock consists of adults. With geese, the goslings can be introduced earlier, although you will have to keep an eye on how the flock reacts to them.

  The best way to introduce new birds is with the help of a portable fence. You can place the new birds in the fence and let the existing flock get used to them. You can slowly open the area up to allow the birds to mingle with one another. Start with about half an hour and gradually increase the time together as the flock gets more familiar with the new birds.

  If you raise the birds from the same age together, the pecking order is formed with less stress and fights. However, unless the birds are violent, allow them to decide who stands where in this order.

When the pecking order is fully established, the meeker birds will voluntarily stay away from the bullies and will stay close to those they are comfortable with. That way the social structure is more peaceful and well-coordinated.

7. Geese and other household pets

If you have dogs and cats at home, then it is best that you find separate enclosures for your geese. While dogs can be trained to protect a flock of geese, you cannot really expect them to have deep friendships given the fact that they have a natural predator-prey order.

Cats can suffer serious damage if they upset a fierce gander. It is also possible that younger goslings are killed by your pet cat.

The best option is to make sure that all the meetings between your household pets and the geese are supervised. You can even place your geese inside a temporary enclosure when your pets are out in the pasture or the backyard.

While it is possible that they coexist without any problem, this is not a risk that is worth taking. Remember that geese are also naturally inclined to fight canine and feline predators. Since they are large birds, an attack can be vicious and even fatal for smaller dogs and cats.

Any introduction should be controlled, with proper enclosures to make it stress free for all the animals. You will also be in better control if you are not familiar with geese and their behavior.

Chapter 3: Caring for a Goose

Once your goose is home, you need to make sure that you provide him with the right care to ensure that your pet is healthy, happy and safe. Like all pets, geese have certain requirements that you need to fulfill.

1. Housing

Geese require a proper shelter so that you can keep them safe from the changes in weather and also from possible attacks from predators. It is advisable that you make the necessary arrangements for your geese before you bring them home so that you can get them straight into their shelter.

a. The right enclosure

The good news with geese is that housing is not very complicated. All you need to ensure is that they have ample sleeping space. On an average about 2 sq.ft per adult bird is what you will need for the flock.

The enclosure that you place your bird in needs to be free from any dampness or draughts. The best option with geese is an enclosure that has a lockable door and is fully draught-free. This will keep them safe from predators and also from the chance of being stolen or harmed by humans.

You will notice that herding geese into the enclosure is not the easiest thing to do. This is because the birds prefer to stay outdoors. That said, having some grains as incentives for the birds inside the enclosure can be of great assistance.

You must line the flooring of the enclosure with sawdust, wood shavings and hemcore that will absorb the smell of the birds' droppings. Without the bedding, the whole enclosure will smell of ammonia. It is never a good idea to use hay as the bedding material, as it will lead to several respiratory infections because of the spores that may be present.

The enclosure must have nesting boxes that are lined with shavings and straw. The nesting box should be cleaned regularly, as the birds may leave droppings in the nest box even when they are laying eggs. When left unattended, the damp bedding can lead to infections in goslings.

b. Keeping geese in a pasture

Geese will love being on a pasture, as they can graze all day. With enough space, you can even feed them on grass that grows on your pasture. They will forage around and eat worms, slugs and bugs. The ideal grazing area for geese is one that does not have grass that is more than 4 inches long.

If the grass in your pasture is too long, it is a good idea to allow sheep or cattle, if you have any, to graze on it before the geese are allowed to graze. If you do not have any cattle, mowing the pasture is strongly recommended.

If you do not have a lot of grass for your birds to forage in, you will have to ensure that they have ample supplements to fulfill their nutritional requirements.

The requirement of pasture space depends upon the climatic conditions in the area that you live in and the quality of grass that grows on your pasture.

Here are a few general rules in terms of the space required for different utility birds:

- Heavy breeding stock: You can have about 5 birds per acre
- Light breeding stock: It is permissible to allow about 6 per acre
- Growers: You can have about 250 per acre for these market geese

The pasture that you are raising geese on should be enclosed with some form of fencing. You can choose any fox proof fencing or electric fencing. Usually, geese are able to protect themselves. However, their vulnerability to foxes means that the area must be covered.

Even if the area that you live in is not really a predator rich area, you must remember that geese tend to wander off quite easily. That means that you have to keep them in a safe enclosure when they are not under supervision.

In the next section we will discuss at length the choices that you have with fencing. Each type of fencing has a unique purpose and you can choose as per the requirements of the flock that you have.

2. Fencing

Poultry fencing is a fundamental requirement when you have geese in your backyard or on a pasture. Foxes can be extremely determined when it comes to getting to your flock.

If you have a pet, it can be extremely disturbing to find out that your bird has been killed or taken away by predators. If you have geese on your farm for commercial purposes, this is definitely a huge economic loss.

The fencing should be very sturdy and well planned. A fox can get over a fence that is about 5 feet in height. If the main threat in your area is a badger, you will notice that they are great at digging under a fence. So, you will have to choose an enclosure based on the kind of predator that you are trying to ward off.

a. Preventing predators

If you have had regular escapes, simple ideas like clipping the wings can be very useful.

The biggest issue that you will face is keeping a predator out. Never underestimate a predator like a fox. Though they look and are perceived to be similar to dogs, they can climb over a fence or just jump over it very easily if they want to get to your flock. The options that you have with respect to fences to prevent predators are as follows:

- Electric netting: This is an ideal type of fencing, provided there is no chance of a short circuit because of long grass. You must also avoid this fencing in areas that have children playing in it. If your area is suitable for electric netting, it is the best option, as it is portable and can be moved to areas where the geese have access to fresh grass.

- Triple wire fencing: This is a secure form of low fencing that can also include an electrical wire at the base. This will prevent any digging and will stop predators that will climb over it as well.

There are several quality grades for the wiring. Getting strong netting will also ensure that the predator cannot tear through the fence. If you notice that the predator is trying to tear through the fence, it is a good idea to double it up.

A large fox can be kept out if your fence is about 6 feet in height. Turning the top upwards and running an electric strand on top will also help prevent any climbing. Make sure that the electric strand is high enough to keep children from reaching it. In places that have a high incidence of fox attacks, a fence that is less than 5 meters is not recommended.

Foxes are known to dig through areas where the ground is soft. Badgers are also extremely good at digging and tearing the net apart. If this is the primary issue that you are facing, it is a good idea to have the fencing buried up to about 8 inches into the ground.

Areas with clay soil are not susceptible to digging. On the other hand, if you have sandy soil on your pasture, you will have to bury the fence as deep as you can. The thumb rule is, any ground that humans can dig into easily will be easy for foxes and badgers.

You can even turn the fence up after 8 inches of burying it. Covering the turned up area with rubble and bricks is a great idea. Additionally, you can even cover the wire with soil after it has been dug in.

If badgers are the primary predator, overlaying the fence with an extra layer of netting or having triple wire is a good idea. This will ensure that strong predators like the badgers stay out. Adding an electric wire at the height of the nose of the badger will also help immensely. Insulating the wires is necessary as this type of wiring is low and easy to reach for children as well as your household pets.

Patching the fence up with gravel boards at the bottom is also a good idea. This means that the predator will have to dig deeper to get through. You can also turn the wire out. You may have to peg the wire down after laying the wire on the surface of your pasture for about 24 inches.

b. Netting options

Chicken netting is quite useful to protect geese. This type of netting is also called rabbit wire, as it is used to keep rabbits from digging through and getting to crops.

Across the widest part of the gap or hole in the fence, the netting is about 50mm. These wires are galvanized to make sure that they do not rust.

As mentioned above, there are various grades of chicken netting. You can get cheaper nets that are 2, 3, 4 and 6 feet in width or about 10, 25 and 50 meters lengthwise.

If the predator in your area is a fox, you will need to get netting that will allow you to dig it in at least up to 18 inches while allowing ample height to prevent the predator from getting in.

Agricultural merchants will be able to sell chicken netting to you. You will also be able to find several suppliers online. Buying online is a cheaper option most of the time, as there are regular deals and offers for you to look out for.

If you don't have foxes in your area, you can also opt for portable netting. These nets are meant to keep the birds in a specific area and are not used for predators. This is ideal even when you want to restrain the birds when you are introducing new members into a flock.

c. Fencing a large area

If you have a large pasture that you have to enclose, then a low electric fence is a good idea. With most predators, the first step is for them to investigate the fence to look for the easiest way in. While doing this, if the electric fence even touches their nose, they will not attempt to get close to it.

You also have the option of sheep or pig fencing. This can be installed by a contractor. Although these fences are lower, the option of adding electrical wires makes it the most economical option available to you. The only thing you need to make sure of is that the grass does not short the electric connection, rendering it ineffective.

Of course, fencing is the first step to protecting your flock. You must also make sure that you herd the flock back into their housing areas every night. This housing must be locked to keep the birds additionally secure. If you are unable to lock the coop or housing area each night, getting an automatic door closer is a good idea, as it can be timed as per your convenience.

3. Feeding Geese

Nutrition is very important to prevent some of the most common diseases that they are susceptible to. It is best that you keep the diet of the bird as close to its natural diet as you can.

Geese are mostly herbivores, while some breeds, like the Roman Rufted Goose, may also eat bugs. They eat a variety of different plant material such as roots, leaves and grass. If they have access to water plants, they may consume that as well.

The closer the diet is to their natural one, the better it is. However, when you are domestically raising geese, it is possible that the necessary food is not available. Even in the winter months, you may have to provide them with specialized foods to make sure that all the nutritional requirements are met.

To begin with, let us understand the foods that you must never give your geese:

- Sugary foods, foods rich in starch, fast food, junk food or anything that is bad for humans too.

- Dairy products. Geese do not have the ability to produce the ingredients necessary to digest milk. That means that they will have serious issues like diarrhea and dehydration. If your bird suffers from serious dehydration, it will cause death.

- Cookies, cakes, bread, chips, etc. will lead to serious digestive issues in birds. They should not be offered to them even as treats.

- Processed foods are not recommended for any of your pets.

It is possible for geese to survive on a diet that comprises exclusively of grass. This is possible only when you have ample grass for each goose. Of course, good quality grass is also required.

Grass that is too long is not recommended for geese. You will have to maintain the height of your grass at about 3 inches. If you have a mixed farm system, you can allow cattle to graze on the pasture before the geese are allowed to forage. You can alternatively mow the pasture frequently.

In case your pasture does not have enough clean and good quality grass, it is a good idea to give your geese wheat. Soak it in a bucket of water until it sinks to the bottom. Then, you can be sure that there will not be any rodents that may eat or contaminate the food.

If you are unable to provide grass to your geese, you will need to give them about 200g of fodder per medium sized goose every day.

You also have the option of including several greens and veggies in your goose's food. They simply love foods like cauliflower leaves, cabbage, lettuce, etc. You can even give them cooked parsnips, carrots or potatoes. The taste for vegetables depends upon the geese. While some may enjoy these vegetables, others may just reject them.

You can try new foods in very small quantities just before your geese go back to the coop at night or just when you let them out in the mornings.

In the spring and summer months, when the grass is in abundance, you will rarely need this. If you must provide additional food, you can give your geese wheat or completely dry poultry pellets.

Clean drinking water is mandatory for waterfowl, as it allows the birds to digest the food that they have consumed easily.

The best way to feed your geese other food is to give them ad-lib wheat in a bucket half filled with water. You can give them a hopper containing the pellets. That way they are free to choose the food that they want to consume.

It is a common observation that geese will lay more eggs when they are consuming pellets and wheat. However, this food puts them at the risk of getting obese. Make sure that you do not give them scraps too frequently. While it may be tempting to feed your pet goose savories from the table, it will lead to several health complications if the bird gets obese.

During the breeding season, it is a good idea to give your bird layer pellets. This is a good way of giving them the calcium that they require for their diet. Layer pellets, however, tend to spoil quite easily and should only be given to them when they are eating the regular meal. Storing it in a hopper gives it the slight chance of getting moist. That will lead to spoiling almost instantly.

To aid digestion, especially in younger goslings, you can give them poultry grit that mostly contains oyster shells. The best way to provide this is with a flower pot that is buried in the ground and then filled with grit. Making a few holes in the bottom is recommended, as it allows the grit to drain during monsoons or humid weather.

Vitamin deficiency is common when you do not give your bird ample food. That will lead to health issues like bumblefoot. In case you decide to give your birds supplements, only do so after consulting a veterinarian. An excess of nutrients is also known to cause severe health issues in birds. Maintaining a good balance in the meals is the key to raising a healthy flock. The requirements change as per the age and when the breeding season approaches. You can seek the assistance of your vet to manage the diet of your birds.

Make sure that the food containers are cleaned and changed everyday. If you notice any growth of mold or fungi in the food, change it immediately. The containers should also be checked for droppings of the birds or rodents. Contaminated food is the cause for most health issues in geese and other poultry.

Keep the food covered at night to avoid attracting rodents that not only eat the food but also carry several microorganisms that are a threat to your flock, causing serious illnesses.

4. Keeping them clean

Making sure that your geese are clean and that their surroundings are clean as well provides a healthier growing environment.

a. Bathing and dusting

With waterfowl, bathing them is not really of much concern to the owners. Birds like geese and swans, particularly, like to keep themselves clean and will do so on the surface of the water that they are swimming in. They may also take a dip in the water and ruffle their feathers to clean them out. Therefore, providing at least a small makeshift pool for the birds is a good idea.

In an event that water is unavailable to them, geese will dust themselves on the ground. Dusting is known to not only clean the bird but also prevent several skin problems. It helps them keep lice in check and will also help keep the skin well-nourished, as the oil glands are stimulated when they dust themselves. If your bird dust bathes himself after a water bath, it could be an attempt to overcome a parasitic infection. In addition, the more the bird works on dusting and bathing himself, the more it suggests that he is not being maintained properly. That will require you to keep the surroundings cleaner.

Bathing constitutes several movements. First, the bird will wade through the water. Then, the goose will stand in the water and fluff the feathers so that the bare skin is exposed. Then, the bird will flick their wings through the water.

The breast remains submerged while the bird rolls back and forth. The bird will then throw his head back while making a cup, with the wings kept elevated. The feathers of the back are then doused. While the feathers are elevated, the water will reach deep into the skin. This sequence will be repeated until the bird is fully clean.

This is followed by preening, where the bird will comb through the feathers using the beak. This releases the oil in the feathers and also helps make them waterproof. They also rearrange the feathers that are quite ruffled and messy after the bath.

The feathers are exposed when the bird is preening. This allows you to assess the quality of the feathers, the colors, etc. You will be able to assess the health of the bird with the quality of feathers.

If there is excessive feather shedding when the bird is preening, it might indicate a nutritional deficiency. In addition to that, it could also be because the bird is molting. Consult your vet if you see the feathers being shed unusually.

You must never bathe your goose with soap, as it leads to skin infection. The only assistance that you can provide your bird with is when the feathers are matted or if there is any debris that will not go away with bathing in the pond.

In that case, you can use a brush to gently remove any matted areas on the feather. Wet the feathers and brush in the direction of the feather growth.

b. Cleaning the shelter
The first thing you need to make sure with the housing area is that it must have ample drainage. Building the housing area on an elevated area is one of the best measures to keep it from having any build-up of moisture.

It is best that you clean out the feeding and watering containers on a daily basis. The food and water must be replaced to prevent the bird from eating any moldy or spoiled food.

At least once a week, the litter and the bedding material should be changed. In case you notice any dampness in the bedding, it needs to be changed immediately. Damp areas encourage the growth of fungi. They are the primary cause for respiratory issues and skin troubles in birds.

To clean the shelter thoroughly, you have to start by dusting and dry cleaning. You will have to sweep the floor of the coop and dust off the ceilings.

All the fixtures, nest boxes, air inlets and fans must be dusted. The feed from the feeders should be removed. Any feces and debris is scraped off the floor and the perches. You can even vacuum the floor as an option.

The power should be turned off before you wet the coop. There are three steps that you can follow:

- **Soaking:** Any area that is heavily soiled can be soaked with a low pressure sprayer. Until the manure and dirt is softened, keep it soaked so you can remove it easily.

- **Washing:** All the surfaces in the building should be cleaned out fully. Focus on the ceiling trusses, the wall sills, the window sills and any area where dust may accumulate. Use a mild detergent with a pH that ranges between 6 and 8. A mild alkali solution like baking soda solution can be sprayed around to disinfect the coop thoroughly.

- **Rinsing:** Rinsing the soap off completely before you allow it to dry is a good idea. Use plain water to rinse and make sure that there aren't any puddles left behind in the shelter.

The shelter can be allowed to dry by air-drying the building. All the windows and vents should be opened. It is a good idea to use a fan or a blower if possible. The best option is to clean when the weather is warm and sunny. This improves the drying process.

Any repairs in the area should be made before you disinfect the shelter one final time. The rodent holes should be sealed, lighting fixtures must be repaired and any breakages or protruding areas in the construction must be repaired.

The most crucial step is the final disinfection, which is usually overlooked by those who have a small flock. Once the whole shelter has been washed, rinsed and dried, you can use a good poultry disinfectant. Your vet will be able to provide you with spray or fumigation options. The best option with most of the small flock shelters is to use a garden spray to disinfect it.

Make sure you follow the instructions provided by the manufacturer with respect to diluting the disinfectant. Usually, you will need about one gallon of the diluted disinfectant per 200 sq.feet of space of the shelter. If you want the process to be more thorough, you can even soak all the feeders and waterers in 200 ppm chlorine solution. You can make that by mixing 1 tablespoon of chlorine bleach in a gallon of boiling water.

With these steps, you should be able to raise a flock that is in the best possible health.

5. Transporting geese

The transportation of geese has several guidelines attached to it. The first thing you need to understand is the regulations in the state or country that you plan to transport your geese to. You can speak to the wildlife authorities in the respective areas for complete details.

When you are transporting geese, the most important things to keep in mind are:

- Preparing the geese for the journey. That means making sure that they have proper containers to travel in and also that there is enough food and water supply for the birds.

- They need to be in good health in order to travel. If you notice any goose having visible health issues, make sure that you do not include them in the travel schedule. It is advised that you have your vet check the birds before they are transported.

- Make sure you check the transport that you will be using, whether it is by rail or road. Ensure that the vehicles are sturdy and in good condition to carry the geese safely.

- Schedule the trip correctly. This will make sure that the geese are delivered and picked up correctly on time. Think of all the situations upon arrival that may compromise the health of your stock.

- Make sure that you pay attention to all the water and food requirements of your geese depending upon the time that the trip will take.

- The birds should have ample space and should be protected from any chance of injury or disease.

Your geese will be at risk if:
- The personnel handling the geese are not competent enough to manage them.

- The birds are not selected properly and unhealthy birds are also included in your trip.

- The duration of the trip is a lot more than you estimated.

- The weather conditions are not conducive for travelling. You need to make sure that you do not travel when the weather is too hot.

- The birds do not have ample space to move around in the vehicle.

- You are unable to observe your birds when they are being transported. That way you will have the ability to take necessary actions in case of any problem.

- The road conditions are not ideal and the terrain is too rough for the vehicle to move on.

- The birds are deprived of water and food for long durations of time.

- The vehicle that you are using is not properly maintained.

When you are transporting your geese, you will need appropriate cages that will allow them ample space to move around. The vehicle should be covered well without any drafts or chances of heating up.

The birds should have enough space to stand up, change positions and lie down when they are being transported.

Make sure that the birds are not deprived of food for more than 24 hours. It is advisable to stop every six hours to give your birds water and a little food. Never keep the water container in the cages. This will lead to possible spilling and dampness.

Make sure that you lift the birds and place them in the cage carefully. They should be placed inside the vehicle in an upright position. Tilting excessively can be stressful to the bird.

The cages must be attached to the vehicle properly to make sure that it does not move around or slide when you are travelling. When getting the birds out of the cage or out of the vehicle, they should never be dropped or thrown out. This can lead to injuries and will also cause a lot of stress to your bird.

In general, travelling is very stressful to geese. There are several factors like the inability to move around freely, changes in the environment, change in the temperature, unfamiliar sights and sounds, improper handling and food or water deprivation that will lead to extreme stress. It is your responsibility to make sure that these possible stressors are avoided.

The cages should be clean and should be made of ridged material. That will ensure that the body parts of the bird do not protrude from these areas when you are travelling. Check the cage for sharp edges, hinges, protrusions or projecting latches. This may cause injuries.

The cages should have ample ventilation while you keep the vehicle free from drafts. Therefore instead of opening windows, turning the air conditioning on is a better idea. If your birds do not have enough space to move around, they will trample one another.

If you have seen that any two birds have had a history of aggression, they should not be kept close to one another when travelling. It is best if you can avoid transporting them altogether.

Ganders that are aggressive should be kept in a cage on their own without the chances of encountering other birds.

The doors and windows should be locked properly. It is also advisable to have proper locking mechanisms on the cage as well. That way, there is no chance of escaping.

It is never advised that you travel for 12 hours continuously. Take breaks to check if the birds are showing any signs of illness or discomfort.

Knowing the history of disease of the birds can be of great use when you are transporting them. That will help you decide if you need to give them any vaccinations or carry out any tests before transporting them. You can consult your vet or any livestock officer before you transport your geese.

Chapter 4: Training your Goose

Like any other pet that you bring home, it is necessary that you have your geese trained properly as well. They should be able to adjust to your environment and lifestyle in order for you and your pet to be happy.

The good news is that geese are extremely intelligent birds that can be taught several commands and can even be given training such as house breaking if you are planning to keep them in a residential area.

If you do not take the time and effort to train your bird, you will not be able to truly enjoy the companionship of a pet. You might have heard of birds like parrots performing tricks. Even geese are capable of this if the owner is willing to take the time to teach the bird.

The only way you can truly train your goose is by being consistent in your approach. You need to understand that this is a lot more time consuming with geese and will require you to completely understand the behavior of your birds.

Even if you have had geese in the past, never assume that two birds are the same. While one of them will learn a command in ten sessions, another one may take up to ten more sessions to learn the same. The main thing you need to do is to teach your goose to learn. When they do learn to learn, you will find it very easy to teach them new tricks.

It is better that you start young and begin by training young goslings. Then, you can work consistently until the bird reaches adulthood.

It is quite simple to distract goslings from any bad behavior in comparison to an adult. However, that does not mean that you cannot work with the adults to achieve the results that you want.

Geese can learn a variety of tricks. Of course, some of them are easier to teach the bird while the others are a little hard to teach the bird. The same applies with the bird itself. Some are ardent learners while the others may put up a fight before you actually get them to do something you want them to do.

House geese can be a new concept to most people, especially the ones visiting your at home. If you have a bird that is unruly and rude and tends to chase, bite or even poop around the place, not everyone who comes to your home is going to be accepting of it.

It is truly the responsibility of the owner to make sure that the birds are well behaved. Once you have them trained well, they can be pleasant creatures. In fact, geese have an awkward way about them that makes them very entertaining to watch as well.

That said, make sure that you are realistic in your expectations. Even with a perfectly trained goose, you cannot attempt things like taking them to a dog park. A dog can kill your bird instantly.

You must also never test the waters when you have children around. Children will be loud and may even attempt to do things like sitting on the goose, which will lead to reactions that are not entirely pleasant.

If you do see that your goose is around any child who is unattended, you must make sure that the goose is taken away. You must also ask the consent of the parents before allowing your bird too close to a child.

1. The manipulative goose

When you are interacting with your geese, try to understand what exactly the bird is learning. Is your bird actually learning about what behavior is expected of him or is he learning how to manipulate you? Geese are a lot smarter than what we believe. Please note that the goose will be referred to as "he" from now on.

You can make sure that your bird does not become manipulative by being consistent. When your bird does anything that you don't approve of, saying "No" each time is mandatory. The no should be assertive. If you laugh when your bird shows any bad behavior, he will thing that his actions are actually pleasing you and will continue to do it.

Train the whole family to use the same words and actions to shape the behavior of the bird. Even the children in your home can train the birds with you. This will also work beautifully with disciplining the child.

Children should be taught that hitting the bird or punishing them will not provide any results. That will also teach them that troubling the bird will make them behave badly and it can be quite dangerous if continued.

Spending quality time with your geese is very important, just as it is with any other pet. If you bring a goose home, the difficult thing to do would be to retrain him. Any bird or human can be a challenge when you have to start from scratch. But do not accept a "good" or "bad" bird. You can make the changes that you desire with your bird.

There is a lot of work with raising a goose that is your own. The advantages include the fact that you do not have any unwanted surprises with respect to your bird. Of course, until the time you have achieved the balance, be prepared to learn about new behaviors almost on a daily basis.

The kind of affection that you give your bird is also very important. When you have a house goose, you may be tempted to pet him and show him affection like you would a dog or a cat. This, however, is not a good idea, as it will make your bird needy and, in some cases, spoiled.

Occasionally holding and petting your bird can be a good thing. If your bird falls asleep in your lap, it is a great sign. It shows that your bird trusts you and feels secure in your presence.

2. Spoiling goslings

If you bring home a gosling, it is true that their cute and cuddly appearance will tempt you to spoil them silly. These birds simply love to be held and will even follow you around.

They will love to eat from your hand and will be extremely affectionate. However, if you overdo this, chances are that you will have a spoiled bird that is demanding and full of bad behavior such as flapping his wings, biting, etc. If you want to raise a well-mannered bird, maintaining a well-balanced relationship is a must.

You will have to spend a lot of time with the gosling to build the trust that you want. Holding them teaches them to trust humans and will also create a strong bond. But remember that any affection that you provide to your gosling should be directed at training or teaching them what is right.

Even with a little bird, bad behavior is bad behavior. If you let things like nipping or flapping go, the bird will grow up to continue with the same behavior. Except, with a larger bird, these habits will spell trouble. Good behavior begins at a young age and will be the foundation of a good relationship with your bird.

If you do spoil your bird and he is unable to stay in your control, you may have to give him up. Now, sadly, no one wants a poorly behaved bird. So, while you are not keen on having him, no one will be keen to take him with them. This will leave you with a bird that you dislike, leading to poor care. Make sure that you do not put your bird through this trauma.

3. Good manners in geese

Good manners with these birds includes things like not biting or chasing. Even flapping can be a troublesome behavior, as the bird will keep knocking things down in your home. It can also become dangerous if your bird develops the habit of chewing on things. He may chew on an electrical wire and cause himself some serious damage.

It is quite easy to distract your bird when he is doing something you do not want him to. For instance, the moment you catch the bird, say "no" in a very sharp, clean and assertive voice. That will tell your bird to drop the habit right away. This should be repeated until the bird loses the habit.

You may have moments of failure when your bird reverts to an old habit despite consistently training him. That is not a major issue and can be handled with a little bit of patience.

Below are some simple obedience commands that you can teach your goose. Practicing these continuously will also help you get the bird to listen to what you have to say. In the end, everyone wants a bird that is welcoming and happy.

a. Coming on call

This is one of the easiest things to teach your bird. Follow these tips to make your bird familiar with his own name:

- Say the bird's name when you are feeding him.
- Call out to your bird when you have a treat in your hand.
- Say the name of your bird when you pet him.
- If you are leading the bird to a pond or pool, call him by his name.

This will make the bird relate his name to pleasurable activities and will make him run to you whenever you say his name.

b. Stop Thrashing

If your bird is not fond of being held or if he does not want to be in a certain place, then thrashing around is the first thing that he will do. This will resemble the motion of swimming and will also include a lot of stomping or wing flapping.

If you are holding the goose when he begins to thrash, keep your hold on the bird and in a sharp voice, say "Stop!" Repeat this word a few times while you hold on to the bird and stand still. At some point, the bird will cease to thrash around. When he does this, you can move forward and place the bird down.

This can be taught to the bird when you are trying to put a diaper on him. The moment the bird starts thrashing, hold him, stop any movement and say "No". In simple terms, geese do not like being in one place for too long. If you can get them to associate thrashing with being held in one place, chances are that they will stop immediately. Keep the practice going until your bird gets in your arms without moving around too much.

c. Stay

Surprisingly, you can actually get your bird to stay in one place for a little over 30 seconds. This is the time you will need to take the bird away from any threat or to take that holiday picture you always wanted.

This training is only possible with consistency. It is hard to teach your bird to stay, but once taught, it can save your bird from being attacked by a predator, running into glass or sharp objects, etc. It is potentially life-saving.

Place your bird in one area and say the command stay. If your bird stays for five seconds, reward him. Slowly increase this time until your bird is able to stay for at least 30 seconds. This can also avoid any attack on people, children or even other birds in your flock. When you see your bird about to attack, you can simply give him the command.

d. No means no

If you intend to keep your goose indoors, then teaching him that no means no is mandatory. He should understand that no matter what the tone is, when a human says no, he needs to stop whatever it is that he is doing.

It is true that your bird will try to push it just to get some attention from you. He may intensify the action. While it may seem cute at first, it will become extremely difficult to manage.

No can mean several things. To tell your bird specifically what you want him to do, double up the no with another command. For example, if you want the bird not to touch something, say "No" and follow it up with "leave it".

The command no will then help you when you encounter a new behavior and the follow up command will tell the bird exactly what it is that you want from him.

That said, be careful about when you use the word no. You need to only use it in case of bad behavior. Overusing the word has led to situations where the bird believes that it is actually his name!

4. Controlling biting

Aggression is seen in almost all animals. It tends to become intense when the bird is just reaching puberty. Irrespective of the age of the bird, even initial signs of aggression such as wing flapping and nipping must not be encouraged.

If you fail to correct the bird when he begins, he will continue with that behavior for a long time. The first thing that you can do is to hold the goose loosely just under his head. This should be followed by a sharp "No". Even hissing at the bird helps if the behavior is intense.

Keep your hold until the bird surrenders. This is how you will show dominance over your bird. You are holding him from moving towards you or away from you. This is similar to rolling an aggressive dog to his side and holding him until he is relaxed.

Do not release your hold until the bird seems no longer interested in you. The bird will not really leave it there and will test your ability to be dominant by repeating bad behavior. Your reaction will remain the same always.

Whenever you are saying no to your bird, keep firm eye contact. If he is very aggressive, hissing is a way of imitating the natural dominance ritual among these birds. Try the hiss only when necessary. It may even frighten your bird or make him very nervous when you use it while his bad behavior is not exactly intense.

5. Walking on a leash

This is a fun activity that you can enjoy with your geese. Just like any pet, walking your geese can be great physical and mental stimulation for them. If you have managed to get your bird or gosling to follow you around, the process of teaching him to walk on a leash will become extremely simple.

The first step to this training is to make sure that you have the right kind of harness and leash. You can find goose friendly equipment online or even with your vet in some cases.

Now, once you have the harness and leash, make sure that you try it out at home before you take the bird out on the street or in the open. The harness must not come off easily. This can become risky if your bird becomes frightened or if he decides to chase something.

A collar must never be used when you are teaching your bird to walk. This will lead to choking if the bird tries to run away or even escape a dog or predator.

Once you have found a harness that you are comfortable using, you can take your geese out on a leash. If your bird follows you around anyway, a light grip on the leash is good enough to direct your bird. The reason you need a harness even with a bird that sticks by you is to keep him away from danger when you are outdoors.

In case your bird does not really follow you around, the first step would be to train him to do so. You can call out his name and even offer treats to the bird when he walks with you. It is unsafe to take the bird out on a harness until he readily follows you around.

If you notice that the pavement is too hot for you to walk with bare feet, it will be too hot for the bird too. Sometimes his reluctance to walk may stem from a pathway that is too hot. If summers get too hot, do not walk your bird.

6. Jumping through a hoop

This is a fun command that you can teach your bird. It is very entertaining and can be mentally stimulating for the bird as well. To begin with, get a hoop that is big enough for your bird to fit through. For a goose the loop needs to be kept low, as he cannot really fly through it or jump through it.

When you show a bird the treat tell him to "jump through". If your bird tries to walk around the hoop, use the treat to distract him. Make sure that you keep the hoop directly in front of him and use the treat to lure him through. On the first attempt, the bird will just walk through the hoop. You can slowly increase the height of the loop to make him actually jump through it.

Be very generous in your verbal appraisal when the bird manages to get through the hoop. As you keep practicing, the bird will walk through the hoop even when you do not have a treat in the other hand.

These tricks can be improvised upon and the same techniques can be used to teach them different commands. A goose can do pretty much what a dog can do if you remain consistent.

Using a treat is definitely the best option, as it gives you good control over the bird. When your bird is able to execute a command perfectly in the presence of a treat, you can begin to try the command without showing the treat at first and then offering it after the bird executes the command. Lastly, you can try with no treat at all.

Chapter 5: Breeding Geese

If you are interested in breeding geese, it could be because you enjoy it as a hobby to raise little geese or you have a commercial purpose for doing so. The commercial or utility purposes usually include meat or egg production.

In the cases of hobbyists and regular breeders, you will see that they select breeding stock that has a good genetic ability that will allow them to produce goslings that mature early and also grow quickly. In the case of breeders who are looking for meat producing stock, they look for qualities like a compact body that is meaty.

Now, the kind of geese that you choose to breed depends upon what you are looking for from the goslings. However, there are some common qualities that you can look for:

- Geese that are not oversized
- They should be of appropriate age
- The stock should be vigorous, which means that they are able to breed readily
- They should have a record of good fertility
- Overall health should be good.

When you are producing goslings with egg production as the main purpose, it is a good idea to maintain records. This will become a point of reference to tell you which geese from the flock need to be culled.

The geese that you choose to breed must be at least one year old before you allow them to mate. In fact, several farm managers do not allow geese to mate until they are 2 years old. Even though it means that you may lose one year's breeding season, it guarantees a healthier stock.

Commonly, geese will be able to breed until they are 10 years old. However, it is advised that you cull them at the age of 6 for healthier offspring.

1. Mating in geese

The ratio of the number of geese per gander is very important in determining the fertility of the gaggle. However, this depends upon the individual bird. While the more geese, the better, you need to make sure that the hatchability of the egg does not get affected in any case. Keep these rules in mind when you are breeding geese:

• If you are breeding a Chinese breed, do not use more than five geese per gander.

• In the case of the larger and heavier breeds, make sure that the ratio does not exceed three geese to one gander.

Mating on water is preferable for geese, although you do not have to necessarily provide them with any swimming facility. If you do have heavier breeds, having deep water sources is a good idea to help improve their fertility.

It is better that you start mating your geese at least 1 month before the actual season of breeding begins. You see, geese are very selective when it comes to choosing their partners. Only when they are able to find a successful mate will they hold on to their partner for life.

To help your goose select a mate, it is a good idea to enclose the number of birds needed in the ratio of geese to gander in a pen to help them find mates. You can put more than the required number for better results.

After the selection of the mate, if you have to change the mate for some reason (say, the mate died or developed a health condition), then you have to make sure that fretting does not occur because the chosen mate is being replaced. That means you will have to keep the birds as far from each other as possible before you find a suitable mate.

You will rarely have issues with breeding geese. Usually, they are very easy to mate. In some cases, ganders may not mate with a few females in the pen. This is because they are just not the "chosen" ones. This means that hatchability and fertility comes down drastically.

In such cases, you may have to resort to force mating in geese, especially if the purpose of breeding is commercial. Then, you will have to remove the gander from the pen and add more females. Give the females some time to get introduced to one another before you introduce the gander back.

If you have a flock with several males and females, you will have to keep an eye on the behavior of the gander. Like the male of any species, dominance in certain birds is common. You must keep an eye on the bird that is most dominant and the bird that is most submissive. They must both be removed immediately. It is likely that ganders that have been raised together will fight less.

Another phenomenon that you must watch out for is lack of interest in the geese. If you see a gander staying by himself and wandering alone most of the time, it is likely that the eggs produced by breeding him will be infertile.

The ability to produce more offspring and have more clutches of eggs that are of better quality will increase with the age of the gander. Mating itself will increase with time. For instance, a two-year-old gander will mate twice as many times as a one-year-old gander.

Artificial Insemination
If you are rearing heavier breeds of geese artificial insemination is one option that you must consider, because a male cannot mate with more than three females in one season. Since geese only have one mating season, it may become very expensive to maintain your flock when they consume a lot of food but produce a very limited number of clutches each breeding season. You will also need more ganders in your flock.

In many countries, artificial insemination techniques have been used quite successfully. Since you will have to put in some additional work, it also means that you do not have to maintain as many ganders in the flock.

You can easily evaluate the quality of the semen and the fertility of the semen using these techniques:

- The female will lay fully fertile eggs just 3-4 days after the insemination.

- She will be able to lay fertile eggs up to almost 10 days after being inseminated.

- The semen that you collect from the gander is good enough for 12 females in one go.

It is recommended that the semen from the gander is collected every three days. You also have to make sure that the females are inseminated every week or every 6 days for maximum results.

2. Production of eggs in geese

Usually, the best season for egg laying for most breeds is spring between the months of July and September. Chinese breeds are an exception, as they tend to begin laying eggs come winter.

It is recommended that you encourage the production of eggs only during the breeding season, as it enables the birds to produce better quality eggs.

Here are some tips about egg production in geese:

- If you mate a mature female with a 1 year old goose, the hatchability is 20% higher and the fertility is 15% higher.

- Since geese normally lay eggs during the day, it is a good idea to collect the eggs in the afternoon or late morning. That reduces any chance of egg breaking.

- You must never allow the geese to use any swimming area until later in the day. Since eggs are laid early each morning, this runs the risk of losing eggs.

- Of course, swimming is very healthy for breeding geese, as they remain clean and also are able to maintain clean eggs.

- In each clutch, a goose will lay about 15 eggs before she becomes broody.

Stimulating early egg production in geese

There are several methods that you can use to encourage early egg production in your flock of geese:

- **Cross breed and genetic selection:** Knowing different breeds of geese can really help get desirable results. For instance, a Chinese breed produces eggs a lot better than an Emden or a Toulouse breed. However, the size of the body can become a disadvantage.

  If you want to produce a breeding stock that will give you ample egg production, cross breeding a Toulouse or Emden with the Chinese breed is a great idea.

- **Use artificial lighting:** Like all birds, geese require a certain amount of light in order to produce eggs. If you have raised hens, you will be familiar with this process in poultry birds. Use artificial lighting to help your stock produce better light. You will be able to get specific lights that are meant for poultry. Setting this as per the requirement of geese will help immensely.

- **Provide better nutrition:** When you notice that your geese are broody, consult the vet about the right nutrition. Increasing the availability of fresh grass and also providing recommended supplements will come in handy.

It is a good idea to create special coops for brooding geese. In addition, have them checked by a vet if this is the first brooding season. If you do not have a complete health checkup for geese that are brooding, it will affect egg production.

Nest boxes with soft bedding like hay must be used. You can use cartons or even specially made wooden boxes that will allow the brooding goose to move around comfortably and rest.

When you have multiple geese brooding in one season, create boxes that will have at least 50cmx50cm space between every three boxes. You can opt for a secluded area like a shed. It is also possible to spread the nesting boxes around a large yard if you are using one.

3. Incubating goose eggs

Of course, the best option for incubation is natural incubation. That guarantees best percentage of hatching in the eggs. However, when you want to use geese to hatch the eggs in the case of a commercial enterprise, it is wasteful. Basically, you want to avoid any wastage of time hatching while the geese could be laying eggs. If you are pursuing it for a hobby, allow nature to take its course.

The best option to hatch eggs naturally is to use Muscovy ducks, hens, turkeys, and similar birds. The best option for goose egg incubation is Muscovy ducks.

You can even hatch the eggs artificially, but using Muscovy ducks will improve the chances of the eggs being hatched correctly.

Here are some tips on incubating goose eggs:

- Make sure that you collect the eggs four times each day. At least twice a day is a must. As mentioned before, you are likely to collect a bulk of the eggs in the morning when they are actually laid.

- The eggs that you intend to incubate must be stored in cooler temperatures. A 15 degree Centigrade setting is the best. You can opt for air conditioning or you may refrigerate the eggs.

- Make sure that the eggs are turned every day. If you store the eggs for more than seven days without incubation, they are less likely to hatch.

- Make sure you select eggs that are not cracked. Weighing them is a good idea and eggs that are about 140g are ideal. Make sure that the eggs are not over 200g.

- Cleaning the eggs ensures better health in the goslings. You can scrub them with steel wool to remove any fecal matter. If the egg is clean, you can simply wipe it with a cloth that is damp.

- Disinfection of the eggs is a good idea. You can fumigate them as soon as you collect them.

- The period of incubation depends upon the breed that you are raising. In the case of lighter breeds, pipping will occur in about 28 days. In the case of larger breeds, this will take about 36 days.

- It is possible that hatching will take about 3 days to complete.

No matter what method of incubation you choose, handling and cleaning the eggs properly is a must.

Natural incubation

Depending on the size of the breed that you are working with, you can place between 4-6 eggs under a brooding hen. In the case of the Muscovy duck, you have the option of incubating up to 8 eggs at one time.

If you are using hens to incubate the eggs, remember that they cannot turn the eggs themselves because of the size of the eggs. You will have to do this manually whenever the hen leaves the nest to feed.

Once you have incubated the egg for 15 days, you must sprinkle some warm water on them every time you turn them.

After the 10th day of incubation, you can candle the egg irrespective of the bird you choose for incubation. This is a process where you pass the egg under a bright light. If you are able to see an opaque, ball-like structure inside the egg, it means that it is fertile. If there is no such formation, you can discard the egg.

If you are using geese to hatch the eggs, then about 15 eggs are incubated in one go. There is no need to sprinkle the eggs with water if you are using a space where the geese have access to water that they can swim in.

Artificial incubation

With goose eggs, the chances of hatching are very low when you use a machine or any such artificial method of incubation. You need to manage the machine properly to make sure that the eggs have a good chance of hatching.

You can use forced draught machines that need to be maintained at a temperature of about 37.5 degrees Celsius when they are being incubated. The necessary humidity can be obtained using a wet bulb thermometer, which needs to be maintained at 32.2 degrees C until the last day of incubation. You can then increase the temperature to 34 degrees C for the rest of the time. Adjusting ventilation and using a moisture tray is also a good idea.

Any incubator that has slow movement of air is a better option for goose eggs. Those that have fast air movement are unable to distribute air properly on the egg to ensure evaporation is uniform.

Tips for keeping eggs in the incubator

- You can get the best possible results if you turn the eggs at least four times everyday. They should be turned at a 180-degree angle. In the case of chickens, it is a 90-degree angle, and that is one important difference.

- It is best to set the eggs that you want to hatch horizontally.

- If the machine is not full already, ensure that you space the eggs out evenly.

- If the incubator is not 60% full at least, make sure that the temperature of the machine is about 0.2% higher.

- Goose eggs naturally need more water. Therefore, in order to get the best results, you need to sprinkle them with warm water every day.

- After 15 days of being in the incubator, it is a good idea to submerge the eggs completely in water every alternate day. The water that you submerge the eggs in should be 37.5 degrees centigrade exactly when measured.

- In the last week, make sure the eggs are submerged for a minute daily. You also have the option of installing a spray water nozzle that will sprinkle water at that temperature.

Tips to use the hatcher
- You must place the eggs inside the hatcher after 27 days of being incubated. If you have noticed that the eggs hatch before 30 days after laying, you can place them earlier.

- The sprinkling of water on the eggs should occur only when they have been transferred to the hatcher.

- Make sure that that the temperature in the hatching area is kept constant at 37 degrees C. The relative humidity must be maintained at 80%.

- The goslings must be left inside the hatcher for about 2-4 hours before they can be transferred into a brooder.

4. Keeping the incubator clean
Hygiene is a very important part of making sure that you have healthy goslings after the eggs hatch. You have to keep the incubator extremely clean in order to prevent any chance of infection.

Here are some tips to clean the incubator and maintain it well:

- Make sure that all the trays and the incubator itself is clean even when it is not in use.

- Fumigation is one of the best ways to keep the incubator sanitized.

- Useormaldehyde gas, which is obtained by mixing combing potassium permanganate and formalin.

- It is a good idea to use a respiration mask that has a gas cartridge filter to keep you safe while using formaldehyde.

- When you are fumigating the incubator, make sure that you turn the motor off first.

- The amount of potassium permanganate that is required should be placed inside in earthenware. Then, pour the amount of formalin required.

- Usually, the ratio is 25 g of potassium for every 35 ml of 40% formaldehyde solution. This is required for every 1 cubic meter of incubator space.

- The machine should later be allowed to run for 10 whole minutes. Keep the temperature at the normal operation value and increase humidity to its maximum, keeping the door of the incubator closed.

- Before you use the incubator, keep the windows and doors closed. That will allow you to provide enough ventilation to prevent the incubator from being overcome by the fumes of the incubator.

Hygiene is one of the most important things when it comes to hatching the eggs of geese. The slightest infection can spread through the clutch in a few minutes, making it a threat to the goslings. Several cases of severe diseases as well as deaths have been related to poor maintenance of the flock.

Hygiene begins from the time you pick the eggs. Make sure that they are fully cleaned before you actually place them in the incubator. Once they have hatched, you can place the goslings in a brooder, which can just be a simple cardboard box with bedding material.

5. Gender identification in geese

It is possible to identify the gender in geese even when they are just one day old. The method is similar to that of checking the gender of chickens. You have to examine the vent of the bird.

In the case of day old goslings, it is a little tricky and the best thing that you can do is get a qualified poultry sexer. If you do not know how to check this correctly, you may even end up damaging the sexual organs of the bird.

In order to check the gender of the gosling, hold the legs firmly between your index and middle finger on the left hand. Gently hold the neck. You need to keep the breast of the bird facing away from you.

Using the left thumb, press on the abdomen gently. At the same time, push the tail down with the right hand. You have to do this in order to get rid of the bowel contents. That way examining gender will be easier.

When you push the abdomen down, you can open the vent. Separating the vent thereafter will help determine the gender of the bird. The cloaca or the penis of the bird will be exposed, helping you understand if it is a female or male respectively. This process can be risky and should be done only when you have enough experience.

In the case of mature birds that are above 7 months of age, a simple physical examination can help find out the gender of the bird. You will need to have two people to do this, however. One simple way of exposing the penis is just holding the tail back towards the head of the bird.

Then, you need to apply downward pressure on the abdomen with the other hand. The organ will be exposed immediately. You will notice that the penis is white and spiral shaped. In immature birds, it

70

is just a little over 1 cm in length. In the case of the mature birds, it can grow up to 4 cm. Inside the vent, you will see that the surface is smooth. The gander has a vent that is pink in color.

There are a few characteristics of the male and female birds that can help you identify the gender as well:

Gander:

- The body of the bird is larger
- The voice is shrill and high pitched
- The neck of the bird is longer
- The head is larger
- In the case of the Chinese geese, you will see the knob just below the top beak
- When you approach the bird, he tends to move outside the flock.

Goose:
- The cry is harsh and hoarse
- The abdomen of the bird is soft and the pelvic bones are wide to allow them to lay eggs.

Once the birds have been identified, it is a good idea to mark them using a band.

6. Raising baby geese
It is quite simple to raise baby geese. All you need to do is follow a few rules:

- You must never give your baby geese medicated food. The best food that you can give a baby goose is starter feed that that is non-medicated. You have certain brands like Rouge Organic Chick Starter, for example.

- Add electrolyte power and vitamins in the water that the baby geese drink to help them develop well. Remember that baby geese need a lot more water than chickens.

- The temperature is very crucial. The goslings are not great with handling heat. It is a good idea to keep it at about 92 degrees F for the first three days after hatching. Then, you can reduce it to 85 degrees F when they are about 7 days old.

- From then on, you can reduce the temperature by about 5 degrees until all their feathers are fully developed.

- Make sure that the birds are able to escape the heat. If you see that the wings are drooping and the birds are panting, it means that they are very hot.

- The birds should be able to move away if they are too hot. After the birds are out of the brooder, you can give them a heat lamp at night. If the weather is too hot, you can avoid this as well.

- Geese require a lot of shade and should be able to get away from the sun.

- It is a good idea to add some water to the feed, so that they do not choke. In any case, goslings like to eat food that is wet.

- Fresh greens, mealworms and bugs can be used as treats for the birds.

- It is a good idea to add some chopped greens to the water that they will drink. The greens should be fresh. If they are wilted or dirty, then you have to worry about any diseases or infections.

- The water should be fresh and clean. It is a good idea to have a dish that is deep enough for the geese to keep their head submerged. This prevents a condition called sticky eye. The birds are able to clean the nostrils out, too.

- In the case of baby goslings, the feathers are not entirely water proof. They will develop oil glands only when they are a few weeks old. The mother usually oils the feathers of the bird to let them into the water. So, if you are artificially brooding them, make sure that you give them time before they are let into the water.

- For the first two weeks, you should give them a chick waterer. Then, you can have something a little deeper.

- A 2 inch chicken wire should be used for the first two weeks so that the birds cannot get into the water.

- Make sure that the water is changed often.

- When the birds are fully feathered, you can allow them to swim. They should have an easy way to get out of the water, failing which they may drown. Provide ramps that will be easy for them to spot and climb out of.

- When the birds are allowed to swim, the enclosure that you keep them in will get messy. Make sure you change the bedding regularly to avoid fungus growth.

7. Imprinting in geese

If you are raising baby geese, the concept of imprinting will be of great importance to you. Ducks and geese are known for a unique ability that is called imprinting.

Goslings are known as precocial or nidifugous. This means that from the moment they hatch, their eyes are open and their brains are large. This makes them capable of the quality of imprinting.

The quality of imprinting was noticed when baby ducks and geese followed their mother around despite the fact that her energy was extremely low in comparison to the energy of the new born geese who are usually inquisitive, mobile and extremely mobile.

In the 1930's the concept of imprinting was described by Konrad Lorenz after observing his graylag geese.

According to him, there are two kinds of imprinting, filial and sexual. Filial imprinting is when the goslings related to someone as a mother figure. Then, you have sexual imprinting where the geese relate to someone as a mating partner.

Filial imprinting

The first 24-48 hours of the gosling's life is considered a very sensitive period. This is when the gosling will understand that he or she needs to follow the mother. Any large moving creature that the gosling sees first is imprinted as the mother.

The biological explanation for imprinting is not a simple one. It is quite complex and has been extensively researched by Howard Hoffman. He states that when the bird sees the creature that is imprinted as the mother, they receive some stimulation that releases endorphins. The stimulation could be the motion, the texture or the shape of the mother figure. This makes the experience very comforting for the goslings.

If a gosling sees a human, he will believe that he is a human being too. Now, for instance, if your goslings see you in the first 48 hours of being born, you can expect them to follow you around. You know that you have been imprinted as the mother figure with the following signs:

- The geese will walk a few feet away from you when they are with you.

- They expect you to protect them from predators or anything frightening. You will see that they will hide by your feet when they feel threatened.

- They will cling on to you and stay close when they require warmth from you.

If your goslings have seen their mother first, they will relate to geese as their mother figure. While you will be a reliable companion for them, they will only consider a goose their mother figure.

If the gosling has been separated from the mother, you will see that they will follow any goose that they see next, even if it is wild goose that wandered into your property. If you intend to separate the gosling from the mother, make sure that the imprinting does not take place with the mother. If not, you will have to spend a lot of energy to keep your geese from wandering away.

A lot of research has been conducted on the process of imprinting over the years. This has suggested that geese can imprint themselves on light bulbs, large objects in the barn or just about anything. Their behavior traits are determined by the imprint that they have with respect to the mother figure.

Filial imprinting is considered irreversible in most cases. While some breeders have been successful in redirecting the imprint on other birds that are more suitable as a species, it is mostly impossible to change the filial imprint that has developed in birds.

Sexual imprinting

This is a process that tends to occur over some time. It is with respect to the mate that your bird chooses in the future. Basically, this refers to the sexual preference of the goose. While this sexual imprinting is only expressed after the bird attains maturity, it ensures that the bird only mates with his own species.

One thing you need to remember with geese is that they will choose a mate that looks like their 'parent'. That means, if they are imprinted with a human, they will look for a human-looking mate.

This can differ for females, however. They tend to show sexual behaviors towards those that have been reared with them. This could be a goose, a duck or even a human. It is seen that hand reared ganders will choose human beings as their sexual partners.

Sexual imprinting usually takes place in two stages. The geese learn from their parents as well as their siblings. As they observe them, their sexual preference is established, or can change as per the species that they are exposed to.

In most cases, it is easy to expect a goose and gander to mate. However, in other cases, it has been observed that a goose or gander may simply reject a bird that belongs to the same species. This behavior may also occur in the wild, leading to many hybrids and new species of geese and ducks.

Imprinting is very important for anyone who chooses to raise baby geese. This concept will help you understand any peculiar behavior that the bird may be displaying at times.

If the bird has been imprinted on a human being, you need to remember that they will want to stay close to you for about one or two years. After they are mature, they may even become very hostile if you try to keep them away from you or when you keep them with their own species as well. That is why you need to be careful about the type of imprint, filial or sexual, that is formed in the birds.

Chapter 6: Health Problems in Geese

Once you have a flock of geese, it is your responsibility to ensure that they are healthy, whether you are raising them as pets or whether you are raising them for commercial purposes.

This ensures that the flocks that you breed are healthy as well. Besides that, you have to remember that some diseases can even be contagious to human beings. So, the more precautions you take, the better it is for your own health as well.

1. Identifying a sick goose

The first step, of course, is knowing that your goose is unwell. Birds will show some obvious signs, such as a change in appearance or behavior, that will help you understand if they need any immediate medical assistance. Some of the most common signs in a goose that is unwell include:

- Lethargy
- Feathers looking ruffled or unkempt
- Unusual shedding of feathers
- Odd colored feces
- Lameness
- Moving out of the flock for ganders
- Loss of appetite
- Depression
- Anorexia
- Difficulty in breathing
- Weakness
- Immobility
- Sneezing

There are several diseases that are common in geese. Each one has specific symptoms that you need to watch out for. The best way to prevent any disease is to maintain proper hygiene and to be aware of the behavior of your birds. Any deviation from normalcy calls for the attention of a qualified vet.

In the next section, we will discuss in detail about the most common health issues in geese and the best ways to prevent them.

2. Common health problems in geese

a. Aspergillosis

This condition is caused by any fungus that belongs to the genus Aspergilus. The condition is also known as Pulmonary Aspergillosis, as it most commonly affects the lungs of the geese. This condition is also very common in ducks.

Usually, in most types of poultry, the most commonly affected members are the young ones. The embryos can be infected too. However, the maximum risk of infection is when the goslings have just hatched.

Infection is usually caused by an improperly maintained incubator or dirty eggs. The condition can affect the hatcher and the setter if the source is dirty eggs.

The Aspergillus fungi can even penetrate into the egg, thus affecting the embryo.

The most common symptoms of this condition include:

- Inability to breathe normally
- Gasping or accelerated breathing
- Rattling noises when breathing
- Gurgling when breathing
- Depression
- Nervous symptoms
- Diarrhea
- Increased thirst

Mortality rate in the hatchlings is usually very high. Prevention is possible when you follow these steps:

- Make sure that you keep the hatching facility clean.
- Your poultry farm should have a proper sanitation program.

- The eggs that are to be hatched must be cleaned and fumigated before incubating.
- Any litter or feed that is moldy must be removed.
- The brooding or incubating area must be disinfected before use.

Treatment involves the administration of Amphoteciricine-B or Nystatin. In case you are unable to source these medicines immediately, you can also add 5 percent potassium iodine to the water that the geese are consuming for three days from the time you notice symptoms.

After this, you can provide normal water for two days and then carry out a second round of treatment with potassium iodine for three more days. If the symptoms fail to disappear, it is best that you have your flock examined by a vet.

b. Avian Adenovirus
While the exact role of the pathogens is unknown, in several cases of infection in geese Avian Adenovirus belonging to Group 1 has been isolated. The disease is not very problematic in geese. This is possibly why there is no vaccine available for the condition.

The common symptoms of the condition include:

- Anorexia
- Diarrhea
- Dehydration
- Anemia
- Low rate of egg production
- Abnormally shaped eggs
- Egg drop syndrome
- Congestion in the lungs
- Edema

Sometimes the virus may also affect the primary organs of the bird, including the pancreas and the lungs. While the reproductive organs are commonly affected in ducks and chickens, it may be observed in geese as well.

Diagnosis includes the isolation of the virus as well as an electron microscopy of samples collected from the affected goose. This is also a disease that usually affects the younger geese between the time that they hatch and reach puberty. The condition can be prevented by:

- Reducing stress in the birds
- Providing proper nutrition
- Ensuring that you have a good sanitation program.

There are no vaccines available for geese in particular. However, the condition does not affect the bird as severely as it would affect other species of poultry such as chickens.

c. Chlamydiosis

This disease is caused by a bacterial infection. Any disease that is caused by bacteria belonging to the genus *Chlamydophila* is referred to by this name.

This disease is of great significance, as it is easily transmitted to other birds and animals and also humans. So, when you are handling an affected bird, make sure that you take all the methods of precaution including using gloves, washing your hands thoroughly and even using a different set of clothes when handling the affected birds.

The most common symptoms of the condition include:

- Difficulty in breathing
- Conjunctivitis
- Inflammation of the sinus area
- Diarrhea
- Deterioration of the breast muscle of the bird.

Treatment is possible using antibiotics called tertacyclines. There is always the underlying possibility of salmonellosis in some cases. That is why a vet may prescribe a combination of different antibiotics.

Salmonellosis and Chlamydosis can affect humans and, hence, pose a threat. These diseases are considered to be of public health significance. If you have recurring cases of either disease, you will have to eliminate the geese that are infected as per the rules in certain states. It is a good idea to consult your vet to have a proper prevention program for these conditions.

d. Coccidiosis
Geese are normally affected by two types of this condition. One of the most prevalent forms of the disease in geese is renal coccidiosis. The causal factor of this condition is *Emeria truncate,* a type of bacteria.

The other type of coccidiosis that you will see in geese is intestinal coccidiosis. This is less prevalent in geese and is generally caused by a type of bacteria called *Emeria anseris.* In geese, five different species of this bacterium have been isolated when the affected organ is the intestine of the bird.

The degree of infection in geese is lower than other birds like ducks. You also do not have to bear as much economic loss as you would have to if the condition affected a flock of ducks or chickens.

The symptoms of renal coccidiosis are seen in younger geese that are between 3 and 12 weeks of age. The younger the bird, the more susceptible he is. The common symptoms include:

- Weakness
- Whitish appearance of the face
- Sunken eyes
- Drooping wings
- Anorexia
- Dullness
- Depression

If the infection is acute, the rate of mortality is as high as 80% in the birds. However, in the case of mild infections, the birds may even develop immunity against the condition quite easily.

The oocysts in the kidney are located for diagnosis. Sometimes, samples are also collected from the cloaca that is located near the urethra.

In the case of intestinal coccidiosis, mortality is low. This condition usually affects the younger birds. The symptoms include:

- Debility
- Morbidity
- Anorexia
- Tottering when walking
- Diarrhea

The small intestine usually gets filled with a fluid that is reddish brown in color. You will also notice the formation of lesions in the lower and the middle portion of the small intestine. These samples are used to confirm the infection.

Treatment can be provided efficiently with the use of a range of coccidiostats and sulphoamide drugs that are available for both the intestinal and renal coccidiosis.

You can provide the same coccidiostats that are used for other poultry such as chickens if the diet of your geese contain portions of feed that are meant for other types of poultry.

In a recent report presented by the Veterinary University of Hanover in Germany, a list of coccidiostats that are used for chickens are tolerated by geese as well. Some of them include amproplium-ethopabate, amropilum, clopidol-methylbenzoquate, zoalene or DOT, narasin, robendin, sulfoquinoxaline, salinomycin and nicarbazin.

There are some types of medicines like aprinocid that are not recommended for geese or any other waterfowl. Make sure that you consult your vet before providing any medication to your geese. Unless you are an experienced owner, you must never attempt to provide medication to your birds without the advice of an expert.

e. Cryptosproridiosis

This is a disease that is caused by protozoans that belong to the genus *Cryptosporidium.* This can infect the intestines as well as the lungs in waterfowl.

In most commercially raised poultry, this condition is noticed. Most cases are not reported, which has led to the lack of appropriate tools. That is why the incidence of this condition in geese is also on the rise over the last few years, especially in the goose industry.

The common symptoms when the respiratory tract is infected include:

* Depression
* Sneezing
* Difficulty in breathing

When the condition affects the digestive system, mortality is usually higher. The symptoms in this case include:

* Diarrhea
* Fluids oozing from the vents
* Oocysts in the feces
* Abnormal droppings

The fluids that are obtained from the lungs and the feces are examined to confirm respiratory and digestive tract infections respectively.

Unfortunately, the availability of drugs in the case of an Cryptosporidum infection is not high. There is enough evidence to suggest that birds can recover quite quickly, however. If the infection is severe in younger birds, death will occur in just a few days of infection. Birds that do recover develop immunity from the infection.

The most effective way to curb any chances of infection is to maintain good hygiene. Any premises that has housed an infected bird should be cleaned thoroughly to make sure that the chances of any further infection in the flock is controlled efficiently.

f. Derzy's disease

This is a viral infection that is more popularly known as Parvovirus infection because of the causal factor. There are other names such as Goose Hepatitis, Goose plague, Goose influenza, Ascetic Hepatonephritis and Infectious Myocarditis that are used to refer to this condition.

This disease is very contagious and is quite common in younger geese. It has been observed that the incidence of the condition is higher in places where Muscovy ducks have been raised. These birds usually transmit the disease to geese.

When the infection is acute, the mortality rate is 100%. When the birds are affected at a younger age, mortality is high. When they are between 4 and weeks old, the rate of mortality comes down, too.

The symptoms in younger ducks include morbidity and death in 2-5 days of being infected. In older birds, you will observe the following symptoms:

- Anorexia
- Weakness
- Reluctance to walk or move
- Nasal discharge
- Discharge in the eyes
- Swollen uropygial glands
- White diarrhea
- Excessive thirst

Once infected, treatment is usually not effective in birds. In the case of adult birds, any infection will lead to immunity. This can make the offspring passively immune as well. This is observed in geese that are about 2-3 weeks old.

It is recommended that the goslings are provided with a proper vaccination program in order to retain immunity. When the goslings are two weeks old, it is recommended that you have them vaccinated. This will only be effective if the parent flock has been vaccinated too.

If you do not intent to breed your birds, initial vaccination is good enough. However, if breeding is on your agenda, vaccination must be repeated again when the bird are about three weeks away from the breeding season. This vaccination should be repeated three weeks before each clutch is laid. You can also provide the bird with a booster vaccine when they are at the peak of laying eggs.

In case you have not had the parent flock vaccinated, you may consider providing a preventive serum to the goslings before they are 10 days old. This will give them passive immunity. The dose must be repeated again when they are 21 days old.

g. Duck Virus Enteritis
While the name can be misleading, this is a condition that can infect swans, geese and ducks. The condition is acute when the bird is infected. The good news is that the incidence in the case of geese is quite low.

This condition can be transmitted when one infected bird comes into contact with another. It can also be transmitted by carrier birds. If the environment is contaminated, birds may get infected as well.

If a bird has recovered from this disease, they become immune to the herpes virus. The strain of virus that affects geese is notably distinct from the ones that were isolated from a flock of ducks that were infected.

The symptoms of the condition depend largely on the gender and the age of the goose, the level of infection and the extent of exposure to the virus. The symptoms that are most common include:

- Hemorrhage in the body cavities
- Hemorrhage in the tissues
- Vascular eruptions, particularly in the mucous membrane of the digestive tract
- Lesions in the lymphoid tissue

There is no effective treatment procedure for the condition. However, you may consult your vet about vaccines that are useful in preventing the condition.

h. Erysipelas

Infection in the flock is sudden with this disease. It is seen in young and mature birds and is caused by a strain of bacteria called *Erysipelothrix rhusiopathiae.*

The condition is quite economically significant in turkeys. However, there have been several reports of acute infection in geese as well.

This strain of bacterial can infect humans as well. Human beings can be infected through puncture wounds and scratches. This makes it a hazard for those who come into contact with birds that are infected. It can, however, be treated with antibiotics.

The common symptoms of infection include:

- Depression
- Formation of lesions
- Diarrhea
- Sudden death

Fast acting forms of penicillin are considered most affective against this condition. They are usually combined with erysipelas bacterin for better results.

Routine immunization in geese is not necessary since the condition is not very common in them. However, if you reside in an area that has frequent cases of infection, you can choose to vaccinate your bird. Once a bird has recovered from acute infection, it is less likely that they will get infected again, as they develop immunity.

i. Flukes

This is a parasitic infection that is seen in water fowl. There are close to 500 species of this parasite that have been classified under 27 families and 125 genera. Infection is most common in geese that have access to ponds or natural lakes. The intermediate host for the flukes parasite is a type of aquatic snail. Another host is the dragonfly.

Every cavity and tissue of the infected bird is invaded by these parasites. Usually it leads to death and the parasites are discovered only after this.

One strain of flukes will infect the oviduct of the goose. This leads to the appearance of the parasites in the eggs laid by the infected goose.

There is no treatment for the condition as such. The only thing you can do is to remove the bird from environments that can become a source of infection. If you have observed any hosts of the parasite in your area, taking preventive measures is necessary.

j. Fowl Cholera

Also known as Pasteurellosis, this is a disease that affects domestic and wild birds. It is highly contagious and is caused by a strain of bacteria called *Pasteurella multocida.*

Geese are highly susceptible to infection and the rate of mortality is quite high as well. There are no notable symptoms of the condition. Birds that are infected will become morbid and die eventually.

The symptoms of the disease will appear just a few hours before the death of the bird. Localized infections are observed in the birds at post mortem. The parts of the body that are normally damaged are the heart, air sacs and the pericardium.

This is not a condition that is contracted in a hatchery, nor is it transmitted from the parent to the egg. It is normally seen on farms that do not maintain proper hygiene practices. It is also likely that the flock will be infected if they are given a chance to interact with infected wild birds.

If fowl cholera has been noticed in your area in wild or domestic birds of any species, it is a good idea to have your flock vaccinated. An outbreak can be controlled by vaccinating healthy birds. You have the option of choosing from several antibiotics that can either be administered orally or through intramuscular methods.

k. Leucocytozoonosis

This is yet another condition that can be related to parasites. The blood cells of the bird get affected, mostly the white blood cells.

You will also see infection of the internal organs of the birds including the liver, heart, spleen and brain.

If there is an outbreak in your flock, it can have severe economic repercussions. However, the incidence in geese is quite low. The disease is common in Vietnam, Europe and North America where the causal agent, *Leucocytozoon simondi,* is more prevalent.

Diagnosis includes microscopic observation of the blood samples and the tissue sections of the infected birds.

Treatment is usually not effective in geese. There are a few drugs that have been administered to infected birds, but with very little success.

The disease is usually carried by insects, particularly species of diptera. They are usually found near streams. The only way to prevent this condition is to remove the geese from the possible sources of infection. Once the bird has been infected, the chances of recovery are poor.

l. Listeriosis
This is a condition that is normally seen in geese that are raised in temperate areas. The causal factor, *Listeria monocytogenus,* is most prevalent in the temperate parts of the world. It is found in the soil as well as in feces. This is one of the reasons why birds that are raised on pastures are more likely to be exposed to the causal factor.

The symptoms include the formation of necrotic areas in the heart and the liver. In young birds, encephalitis occurs. Diarrhea is the most common symptom of the condition.

The treatment methods for this condition include the removal of the source of infection and administering antibiotics, particularly tetracyclines.

m. Mycoplasma infection
Commonly known as Pleuro-Pneumonia like Organism or PPLA, this is a serious condition in geese. The causal organism has a structure that lies in between viruses and bacteria. There have been more than three species of Mycoplasma that are known to affect geese.

Infection in geese has increased over the years. It is commonly seen in birds that have been raised in conditions that are intensive. In the case of the younger geese, the conditions in which they are hatched seems to be the source of infection.

The common symptoms include:

- Reduced fertility
- Lower egg production
- Necrosis of the phallus area
- Reduced growth in goslings
- Respiratory tract infection.

You can prevent the condition only when at least two generations of geese that are being bred are declared free from infection. In any case, making sure that the eggs are cleaned before hatching can be a preventive measure.

In case you obtain eggs from a flock with a history of infection, you need to dip the eggs in a solution of tylosin before incubating them. If the goslings are infected, adding tylosin or tetracyclines to the drinking water is a great measure to treat the condition.

n. Mycosis in the digestive tract

The causal factor of this condition is *Candida albicans.* The disease is common in birds that are force fed. The corn dispenser that is inserted to feed the bird makes the esophagus infected. The infection becomes a site of entry for the causal agent.

The most common symptoms of the condition include:

- Lesions in the crop
- Whitish deposit in the crop
- Stunted growth
- Ruffled feathers
- Listlessness

If the conditions that the birds are raised in are unhygienic, infection is possible. Overcrowding can also lead to infections. You have to make sure that you provide your geese with a healthy environment to begin with.

Adding copper sulfate to the water that the birds drink has provided significant relief from infection. You can even increase the pH in the crop by adding sodium bicarbonate to the drinking water. This makes it difficult for the organism to thrive. You can even add Amphotericin and Nystatin to water to make sure that your geese are free from infection.

However, this condition is not very common in geese. Nevertheless, maintaining hygienic pasture conditions is a must when you have geese.

o. Mycotoxicoses

If your flock is exposed to mycotoxins, this condition can occur. The most common source of infection is food that is moldy. There are hundreds of mycotoxins that can affect geese. Therefore, diagnosis can be complicated.

In tropical countries, the prevalence of alfatoxins is high. The origin of the condition is related to *Aspergillus* fungi, which is seen in copra, rice barn, corn and soybeans. Another genus called *Fusarium* is known to affect geese commonly. These organisms are usually seen in brewer's grains, sunflower seeds, barley, sorghum and oats. These organisms thrive in areas that are high in humidity and those areas where the temperature is around 24 degree C.

The common symptoms include:

- Refusal to eat
- Reduced levels of activity
- Increased consumption of water
- Reduced hatchability of eggs
- Reduced production of eggs
- Death in case of T-2 toxin infection
- Damage to the testes

Removing contaminated foodstuffs is the best way to prevent the condition. Make sure that your geese have access to fresh foods. It is also advisable that any grains that you are providing are harvested early before fall to prevent the production of mycotoxins, particularly in temperate areas. You can also purchase feed that is mycotoxin free.

p. Necrotic enteritis
This condition is caused by an organism called *Clostridium perfringens.* This organism is usually seen in feed that is contaminated, feces, soil, dust and litter.

The symptoms of the condition include:

- Reduced appetite
- Reluctance to walk or move
- Ruffled feathers
- Severe depression
- Ruffled feathers

The chances of small intestine necrosis are high. This leads to immediate death in the birds. Prevention is the best cure. If your birds are raised in stressful conditions, the chances of infection are high. You will also notice infections if there is any irritation in the digestive tract.

There are several antibiotics that may be administered to infected birds such as nitrovin, avoparcin, virginiamycin, tylosin and penicillin.

q. Nematodes
These are the most common parasites that occur in poultry infections. In case geese are affected by species belonging to the *Capillaria and Heterakis* genus, it can become a health hazard. In the case of geese, infection is usually caused by *Amnidostomum Anseris.*

The most common symptoms are:

- Lethargy
- The presence of roundworms in the feces
- Dark coloration of the gizzard that is only seen when the bird is taken for an autopsy.

Good management is the most effective way to manage nematode infection. In the case of geese, rotating the pasture every 3-4 months is a good idea. This will prevent the chances of re-infection in geese.

If your geese are being raised in confinement, you must make sure that the enclosure is regularly cleaned and disinfected. You should also change the litter regularly. Since younger geese are most prone to infection, it is also a good idea to avoid mixing older and younger geese when raised in confinement.

There are many anthelmintic drugs that you can administer for nematode infections. To treat *Amidostomum* infection, you can use mebendaxole, pyrantel, cambendazole and fenbendazole. You can even include coumaphos and Hygromicin B in the feed to prevent other infections.

r. Nephratic Hemorrhagic enteritis
This condition is also referred to as NEHO and is most commonly seen in geese that are raised in the southern part of France. Infections are most prevalent in birds that are between 4 to 20 weeks of age. The rate of mortality is between 30 to 100 per cent.

The causal factors are not properly known. However, infection is often related to poor management of the flock, sudden changes in the diet, excess protein content in the feed, poor quality of drinking water, etc.

The symptoms include:

• Unsteadiness
• Erratic movement
• Trembling

These symptoms are followed by death. You will notice hemorrhaging and lesions in the kidneys along with swelling in the sub cutaneous areas in the autopsy. You can even see an abnormal presence of parasites in the intestines.

The first step towards controlling infection is good management. You must also ensure that the geese are given a balanced diet.

In case of an outbreak in the flock, the best option is to inject homogolus serum. You can even administer renal detoxicants and tonics that can relieve the symptoms to a large extent. There is no proper understanding of the condition as yet, resulting in a lack of reliable vaccines.

s. Newcastle Disease
This is a viral condition that is very common in most poultry birds. In the case of geese, infection is usually due to *Paramyxoviruses.* The condition does not affect geese severely, which has led to a lack of any vaccination against the condition for these birds.

The clinical signs include:

- Disorders in the central nervous system
- Greenish diarrhea
- Lethargy
- Loss of limb coordination

In most cases, a goose that is infected will not show any symptoms. However, they could be carriers and can be a threat to other birds that are susceptible.

t. Paratyphoid
Salmonellosis or paratyphoid is a very important health condition with respect to geese. Usually, birds that that are less than six weeks of age are most susceptible to infections.

The condition is also a cause for concern because it can affect human beings. There has been a demand for poultry products that are salmonella free, leading to the inclusion of monitoring programs in many countries.

There are close to 2000 types of salmonella organisms that are known to affect poultry birds. The type of organism that affects a bird or flock depends on the region that the birds are raised in.

The condition is spread when an infected bird comes into contact with a healthy bird. It is also possible that the infection is transmitted through equipment that is infected, the soil and feces.

Most infections are caused by poor management of the hatcher and brooder.

Salmonella can also occur in eggs and can multiply rapidly after entering an egg. Therefore, you need to make sure that you collect the eggs quickly as they are laid. You also need to make sure that the eggs are properly fumigated and cleaned before being transferred to the incubator.

The most common symptoms include:
- Increased water consumption
- Anorexia
- Diarrhea
- Pasty vent area
- Lowering of the head
- Eyes closed
- Ruffled feathers
- Dropped wings
- Huddling close to a source of heat.

Removing the sources of infection is the first step to prevention of an outbreak. You need to make sure that your pasture or enclosure is clean and well managed.

The hatching process is also crucial and you need to make sure that only clean and healthy eggs are hatched. Controlling the entry of rodents into the enclosure of the geese is also an important step towards the prevention of the condition.

The drugs that are administered for treatment depends largely on the source of infection. You have the option of several antibiotics, sulphonamides and nirtofurans. You can also choose to inject gentamicin or specticomycin as part of the treatment process depending upon the actual causal factor of the condition in your flock.

u. Riemerella Anatipestifer Infection

Riemerella Anatipestifer infection is very contagious in domestic geese. The birds can be infected by other species of poultry or waterfowl.

The most common symptoms include:

- Coughing
- Sneezing
- Green colored diarrhea
- Nasal discharge
- Discharge from the eyes
- Uncoordinated movement
- Tremors in the neck and head
- Coma

A goose that recovers from the condition becomes immune in most cases. Treatment includes the administration of antibiotics and sulphonamides. There are certain vaccines that are available. They are primarily used to treat the condition in ducks, although they are considered to be effective in the case of geese as well.

v. Pseudotuberculosis

This condition is caused by an organism called *Yersinia psuedotuberculosis.* It is seen in swans quite commonly and rarely in ducks.

The common symptoms include:

- Inability to walk
- Ruffled feathers
- Diarrhea
- Dull feathers
- Difficulty in breathing
- Weakness

Usually streptomycin, tetracycline and chloramphenicol are administered to treat the condition.

w. Spirochetosis

This is a tick borne condition that is caused by an organism called *Borrelia anserine*. It is a severe disease that was first described in the year 1891. The condition is prevalent in the tropical and temperate areas where fowl ticks are common.

Mortality in affected birds can range from 2% to 100%. It is seen that with constant exposure and recovery, birds develop immunity. Any puncture on the body or bites from ticks can form the first step for diagnosis.

Vaccination is available as a preventive measure. Geese that are immune due to vaccination or due to exposure to the organism can pass on passive immunity to their progeny. This will keep them protected for up to six weeks from hatching.

In case of an outburst, antibiotics are prescribed. The best options include tetracyclines, tylosin and penicillin. The causal organism is very sensitive to most of these antibiotics.

x. Tapeworms

There are close to 1400 species of tapeworms that can affect wild and domestic birds. There have been some records of intermediate hosts in most cases.

Where the intermediate host is known, removal of the host is the most effective preventive measure. In the case of geese, you will notice high incidence in birds that have access to natural lakes and ponds, as they may come into contact with an intermediate host.

If the goose is infected you will see lethargy and reduced performance. However, more accurate diagnosis is only possible when the worm is identified and isolated.

While geese do not contract tapeworms easily, it is a good idea to keep them away from possible hosts. In case of an infection, drugs like butynorate are most effective in treating the infection.

y. Trichonomoniasis

This is a condition that is caused by a protozoan called *Trichomonas gallinae*. It is mostly seen in flocks that are breeding. It can be transmitted from one bird to another or through the drinking water and food. If the infection is heavy, the rate of mortality can be high.

The common symptoms include:

- Weight loss
- Reduced performance in reproduction
- Reduce ability to lay eggs
- Unusual droppings

The first step to preventing an outbreak is to isolate a bird that is infected. Medicines like metronidazole and nitrofurazon are effective in treatment.

z. Venereal diseases

Certain strains of bacteria such as *Candida, Mycoplasma and Neisseria* can lead to venereal diseases in ganders. The primary infections are caused by *Mycoplasma.*

The symptoms include:

- Swelling in the phallus
- Inflammation of the cloaca
- Necrosis in the phallus
- Scarring
- Ulceration
- Inability to reproduce

This condition will spread rapidly in the flock. It usually spreads via the female. Proper management of the breeder stock can prevent infection. You also have the option of administering antibiotics like tetracycline and tylosin to birds that are infected.

3. Addressing Bumblefoot

We are discussing bumblefoot as a separate section because of the rate of incidence and the extreme effects that it can have on the birds. This is a very common condition in domestically raised birds and can spread in the flock very easily.

The condition occurs in different stages and can range from mild soreness in the feet to inability to move. You need to make sure that you take all the necessary precautions to prevent bumblefoot in your flock.

a. Stages of Bumblefoot

There are various stages of bumblefoot that you must keep an eye out for:

- **The first stage:** In the initial stages, you will notice a formation of pink colored calluses on the foot of the bird. They are seen on the lower surface of the feet and are very hard to the touch. In most cases, both feet will be affected.

  These calluses appear as shiny patches or reddish areas that may spread to the top of the feet as well. This is usually caused when the surface the birds rest on or perch upon are hard and rough.

- **Second stage:** When the condition reaches the second stage, the protective out layer made of scales disappears. This allows bacteria like the staphylococcus to come into contact with the bird, leading to infection.

  The sores on the feet become more inflamed and red in color. You will need to administer some antibiotics when the infection reaches this stage. You will also need to determine what caused the primary infection to make sure that the condition does not elevate to the third stage.

- **Third stage:** In the third stage, you will see notable discomfort in the bird. The reddish sores will become black or blue in appearance. The feet become distorted and may result in permanent damage to the feet.

  You will notice that your birds will lift up their feet in order to relieve the discomfort. If you allow the condition to elevate, severe lameness is caused and the only chance of recovery would be surgery.

b. Confirming bumblefoot

Sometimes it is possible to wrongly diagnose a condition to be bumblefoot. Here are some tips to ensure that your bird has bumblefoot:

- If just one leg is affected, it is possible that the bird has had some localized infection. There may also be some injury that the bird is suffering from.

- If the legs seem to be dry or scaly, the condition could be entirely different. This is not a good sign and requires medical attention.

c. Causal factors and control

There are several options to control the condition. Your vet may prescribe antibiotics, hot soaks, or a change in the bird's diet. If the condition gets very severe, you may have to opt for surgery. Surgical procedures are needed when the foot is severely damaged or distorted. This will prevent complete lameness in the bird.

The most common causes are:

- Perches and surfaces: The standing and walking areas are unsuitable, such as being made from plastic or rough material. If you are using perches, they should be varied in texture.

  It is a good idea to give your bird access to natural perches that have different surfaces, textures and circumferences. You can encourage the bird to walk around more by placing his food bowl in various places.

  If the floor is wired or hard, you should make sure that there is some bedding or litter. That will make it easy for the bird to walk on the surface and also heal in the initial stages of bumblefoot.

- Infections: If the bird has had any injury or cut, it becomes very easy for an infection to occur. So, any cut or injury that you notice must be treated at the earliest. If the infection becomes severe, you may have to administer antibiotics.

If you are applying any antibiotics topically, make sure that you clean the lesion completely. It is a good idea to soak the foot in warm water with Epsom salt. This helps remove scabs and debris.

Lastly, you can wash the wound with some hydrogen peroxide. That will destroy any bacteria in the area. The wound must be cleaned completely to keep it clean. Repeat this dressing at least twice everyday.

Any infection that is left untreated can enter the bone and even infect other parts of the body. This can be life threatening.

- Poor nutrition: If the diet of the bird is poor, it can lead to obesity or malnutrition. Any diet that is high in protein and cholesterol is fatty. If the diet is low in calcium as well, it can cause bumblefoot.

The most common cause for bumble foot is a deficiency of Vitamin A. You will notice that the feathers above the nostrils are stained if there is a deficiency. This shows that nasal discharge has occurred in the bird.

You will see more subtle signs like dullness in feathers, coloration of the beak and legs, etc. You can provide supplements to your birds and they respond to it quite well. You can also add foods like dark leafy vegetables to your birds' diet.

Stored proteins can also cause bumblefoot in birds. The internal bacteria that tend to be excreted will grow when using stored proteins. These bacteria tend to infect the bare areas such as the feet, causing issues like bumblefoot. If bumblefoot is caused by an excess protein level, you will normally see the first signs of infection on the bottom of the foot.

The only way to curb infection is to reduce protein content in the diet of your bird.

- If you notice that only one member of your flock is suffering from the condition, it is most likely not bumblefoot. Especially when the other birds are about the same age and are in the same enclosure, the appearance of redness and pinkness could be triggered by an infection, lack of nutrients or excessive uric acid in the bird's body.

4. Control and prevention of common diseases

Here are some tips that will help you keep your flock free from any diseases:

- The geese should be examined completely before you buy them from the breeder. Make sure that you only opt for reliable sources when it comes to breeders.
- You need to give your new geese adequate access to good quality water and food.
- The troughs and water containers should be kept clean and free from any contamination.
- The environment should be stress free. That means that it should be free from any noise or other disturbing elements like predators.
- Make sure that you do not add birds that have been obtained from a different source to your flock. Instead, you may opt to make another flock altogether.
- Breeders should be kept away from the geese that are growing.
- The golden rule with geese is that the younger they are, the more susceptible they are to health issues. Therefore, keeping birds of different age groups is never recommended.
- Make sure that your flock has access to regular vaccinations and medicines. You must always give them medicines and vaccinations only after you have consulted a vet. Wrong medication can lead to serious issues in birds.
- Whenever you are inspecting your flock, start from the youngest and then move to the oldest. The youngest ones are the ones that are likely to have the most number of symptoms.
- If you find a goose that is unwell, make sure that you isolate him immediately. Until the condition has been completely diagnosed, there is no way of knowing if it can harm your flock in any way.

- In case of any death in your flock, ensure that the goose that is dead is incinerated or buried properly. It is also recommended that you get a diagnostic report at the earliest. The samples from the carcass can be sent to the vet to determine the cause of the bird's death.
- If you have visitors on your farm regularly, make sure that they do not meet the geese without any protective clothing. You must also ensure that visitors have not been around any geese for at least 14 years before visiting your flock.
- If you are selling the geese that you breed on your farm, make sure that they are not taken out on crates that are unclean and unhygienic.
- If you have multiple flocks on your farm, ensure that you keep their housing areas and the area between them sterilized and clean. This reduces the number of organisms that can cause infections to your flock.
- Make sure that you have records of the illnesses or deaths that have occurred on your farm.
- As much as you can, keep any wild bird out of your pasture.

Taking ample measures of precaution can help you save a lot of money that you may have to spend on medical bills and veterinary services otherwise.

5. Finding a good vet

With birds, you need specialized vets to attend to them. While a regular vet will be able to provide you with temporary relief during an emergency, you will need a qualified poultry vet or avian vet who can help care for your flock.

Now, it is not quite as simple to find a poultry vet as it is to find a vet for other pets. When you have a goose as a companion animal, it is natural that you will treat him like any other pet. This means that you will share a close bond and also have additional concerns with respect to the health of the bird.

You need to find a vet who understands your concern for a goose. There have been several pet owners who have talked geese owners down for "caring too much" about the bird. So, when you are in talks with a vet who can potentially become the one to take care of your flock or companion birds, here are a few questions you must ask:

- What is their opinion about having geese at home as companion animals?

- Do they treat geese at the facility, and if so, how often do they work with geese?

- How often do they perform surgical procedures on geese? If they do, what are the facilities available to admit it?

- Do they support the idea of prosthetic coxofemoral joint replacement in geese? If they have no information, they should at least be willing to do some research and find out about the procedure.

- Ask them a little about the antibiotic doses for geese. What is the measure per kilo of body weight?

- What are the vaccination programs available for those who have a flock of geese?

It is best that you find a vet who is a specialist in avian medicine. Special poultry vets who are licensed and have advanced training to help poultry like turkeys, ducks and chickens are the best option.

A poultry vet will be able to carry out the following duties:
- Observing the behavior of the flock
- Conduction routine inspections
- Evaluating the quality of the meat and eggs
- Taking necessary samples to analyze
- Provide advice on nutrition
- Basic examinations
- Providing vaccinations
- Creating a health management system for the flock

Poultry vets work at regular hours and have about five to six days a week of practice. You will find avian vets who have a specific species or areas of interest. You need to find one who specializes in geese. The next classification is the kind of production, whether it is eggs or meat.

A poultry vet would be a Doctor of Veterinary medicine. During this course, they will study large and small animals comprehensively. It is necessary that the vets take an examination that will help them obtain a license to practice.

Those who seek to work with poultry exclusively will obtain additional training by publishing articles, residency programs and may even be sponsored by a poultry veterinarian board. There are specialized colleges such as the American College of Poultry veterinarian that helps certify poultry veterinarians each year.

A good poultry vet may also have affiliations with professional organizations. One such organization is the Association of Avian vets, which also produces a journal of Avian Medicine and Surgery to keep veterinarians updated about new practices and services.

The international division of the above mentioned organization is called the European Committee of Association of Avian Medicine and has members from countries like Dubai, Europe and North Africa.

One such organization that is entirely dedicated to poultry is the World Veterinary Poultry Association. They host a conference every two years that is attended by vets from all over the world.

If your vet is able to attend these conferences or has regular updates through newsletters or journals, your birds are in great hands.

If you are unable to locate a good avian vet, the official websites of these professional organizations will be able to provide you with several leads. You can also speak to a local vet to help you look for a dedicated avian practice facility.

When choosing a vet, make sure that they are easily accessible, will provide farm visits in case of an emergency and also have good inpatient facilities in case your bird requires any surgical procedures to be conducted. Once you find the perfect vet, they will play an important part in raising healthy geese.

6. Injuries and first aid

Besides the above listed emergencies, injuries are also a cause for concern and may require immediate attention from a vet. However, you may not get ample time to take the bird to the vet and will have to administer first aid in order to bring the situation under control. Here are some common injuries and simple tips to deal with them in the most effective way:

- **Broken blood feather:** This can lead to a lot of blood loss. Adding some styptic powder over the affected area can help the bird. Then apply some pressure on the area with gauze. The vet will mostly remove the shaft to make sure that the bleeding stops.

- **Dog and cat attack:** Hold your bird calmly and try to reduce the stress caused by the attack. If there is a wound that is bleeding, hold it down with a piece of gauze.

  In the event of any broken wings, hold the wing close to the body and keep it in place with tape or gauze. Taping too tightly will lead to breathing problems. It must only be tight enough to hold the bird's wing in place.

  If there has been an attack, make sure that the bird is taken to the vet immediately, even if you do not see any visible signs of injuries in the bird. There is always a chance of infection that needs to be examined.

- **Wounds and abrasions**: This can happen when your bird's body rubs against a sharp surface, if your bird walks near thorns, or any such thing. The first thing that you need to do is wash the wound with hydrogen peroxide or betadine. Using a pair of tweezers, get any dirt out of the way. Feathers that are sticking to the wound need to be removed as well. You can apply any antibiotic ointment and allow the wound to heal. The bird must not be allowed to pick at the wound, as it may get deeper.

- **Breathing issues**: If you notice that your bird is straining to breathe, the first thing that you will do is check the nostrils. There could be a foreign object that is blocking the nostrils.

  If the bird is breathing with the mouth open, it means that he is either afraid, exhausted, or overheated. If the wings are outstretched, there is definitely a chance of overheating and you must get the bird to stand on some cool water or on a wet towel.

  If none of the above helps, the bird may have developed breathing issues due to any underlying illnesses.

- **Burns:** The affected area should be washed with running cold water. Then, you can dry the area with some gauze and apply an ice pack. Any extensive or severe burn requires immediate veterinary attention to prevent further injuries. You must provide ample care to these birds, as they may be in a state of shock.

- **Chilling:** Even a sudden drop in temperature can be bad for your bird. The body should be warmed up immediately using a heat lamp or by wrapping it with a warm towel. Be sure to raise the body temperature gradually. The air temperature should be maintained at room temperature to avoid overheating after chilling.

  Determine the cause of overheating. If it is because of any shock or injury, consult your vet. At the same time, check the environment for any drafts. In that case, relocating the bird is the best option available to prevent chilling.

- **Toxication:** Toxins may be inhaled, in which case the bird must be moved to an area with good ventilation immediately. If the bird has only had physical contact with the toxin in the form of a spray, you must bathe him immediately. Ingestion of toxins is always a major cause for concern. Make sure you consult the vet immediately. If you call the poison control center in your locality, you will have to provide details like the name of the toxins, the amount consumed, the symptoms exhibited by the bird and more.

It is a good idea to make sure that your home is stocked with a first aid kit containing the following items in order to provide proper, timely help to your pet:

- Phone number of the vet and directions to the clinic
- Emergency numbers in case of non-availability of the regular vet
- Poison control numbers
- A pair of scissors to cut the bandage material
- Sterilized gauze pad to apply pressure on the wound if it is bleeding and to clean the wounds
- Q-tips to apply ointments
- Tape of gauze roll to wrap the animal in case of an injury
- Antibiotic ointment recommended by the vet
- Hydrogen peroxide to clean the wounds
- Pliers to remove wires or debris
- Thermometer
- Heating pad or lamp to maintain the bird's body temperature
- Large towels to wrap and pick up the bird when needed
- Syringe and medicine dropper.

You can talk to your vet to create an emergency program for your flock as well. First aid that is provided in time can prevent lot of issues.

Conclusion

I hope that you have been able to get some insight into the responsibility of bringing a goose home.

If you have been able to seek answers to some common questions about raising geese, then I consider my work done.

In order to reach out to several others who want to learn about raising geese, we require constant feedback from our readers. Do let us know what you liked or disliked about the book so that we can make the necessary amendments to bring you nothing but the best pet care.

References

Keeping yourself updated about goose care is one of the best ways to be a good parent to your bird. The Internet is one of the best places to seek information. Here are some websites that are extremely informative. They are also updated regularly to ensure that you are in sync with the trends.

http://www.animalwelfarestandards.net.au/

www.nswschoolanimals.com

www.housegoose.com

http://www.backyardchickens.com/

web.stanford.edu

http://www.duckhealth.com/

https://poultrykeeper.com

www.beautyofbirds.com

www.chickens.allotment-garden.org

www.dpi.nsw.gov.au

www.eoursesonline.iasri.res.in

www.aussieslivingsimply.com.au

www.articles.extension.org

www.buffganzen.nl

www.goodmansgeese.co.uk

www.pet-health.knoji.com

www.goosebusters.net

www.grangecoop.com

www.raisinggeese.com

www.hobbyfarms.com

Printed in Great Britain
by Amazon